S0-AYP-947

Building Wealth
through Venture Capital

Building Wealth through Venture Capital

A PRACTICAL GUIDE FOR INVESTORS
AND THE ENTREPRENEURS THEY FUND

Leonard A. Batterson
Kenneth M. Freeman

WILEY

Copyright © 2017 by John Wiley & Sons, Inc. All rights reserved.

Published by John Wiley & Sons, Inc., Hoboken, New Jersey.
Published simultaneously in Canada.

No part of this publication may be reproduced, stored in a retrieval system, or transmitted in any form or by any means, electronic, mechanical, photocopying, recording, scanning, or otherwise, except as permitted under Section 107 or 108 of the 1976 United States Copyright Act, without either the prior written permission of the Publisher, or authorization through payment of the appropriate per-copy fee to the Copyright Clearance Center, Inc., 222 Rosewood Drive, Danvers, MA 01923, (978) 750-8400, fax (978) 646-8600, or on the Web at www.copyright.com. Requests to the Publisher for permission should be addressed to the Permissions Department, John Wiley & Sons, Inc., 111 River Street, Hoboken, NJ 07030, (201) 748-6011, fax (201) 748-6008, or online at www.wiley.com/go/permissions.

Limit of Liability/Disclaimer of Warranty: While the publisher and author have used their best efforts in preparing this book, they make no representations or warranties with respect to the accuracy or completeness of the contents of this book and specifically disclaim any implied warranties of merchantability or fitness for a particular purpose. No warranty may be created or extended by sales representatives or written sales materials. The advice and strategies contained herein may not be suitable for your situation. You should consult with a professional where appropriate. Neither the publisher nor author shall be liable for any loss of profit or any other commercial damages, including but not limited to special, incidental, consequential, or other damages.

For general information on our other products and services or for technical support, please contact our Customer Care Department within the United States at (800) 762-2974, outside the United States at (317) 572-3993, or fax (317) 572-4002.

Wiley publishes in a variety of print and electronic formats and by print-on-demand. Some material included with standard print versions of this book may not be included in e-books or in print-on-demand. If this book refers to media such as a CD or DVD that is not included in the version you purchased, you may download this material at http://booksupport.wiley.com. For more information about Wiley products, visit www.wiley.com.

Library of Congress Cataloging-in-Publication Data

Names: Batterson, Leonard A., 1944– author. | Freeman, Kenneth M., 1949– author.
Title: Building wealth through venture capital : a practical guide for investors and the entrepreneurs they fund / by Leonard A. Batterson, Kenneth M. Freeman.
Description: Hoboken : Wiley, [2017] | Includes index. |
Identifiers: LCCN 2017016750 (print) | LCCN 2017020511 (ebook) | ISBN 9781119409373 (pdf) | ISBN 9781119409366 (epub) | ISBN 9781119409359 (cloth)
Subjects: LCSH: Venture capital. | Investments. | Business enterprises—Finance.
Classification: LCC HG4751 (ebook) | LCC HG4751 .B368 2017 (print) | DDC 332/.04154—dc23
LC record available at https://lccn.loc.gov/2017016750

Cover Design: Wiley
Cover Image: © norph /Shutterstock

Printed in the United States of America.

10 9 8 7 6 5 4 3 2 1

Contents

Preface

While taking some time off after selling his Chicago-based company, MusicNow, to Circuit City in 2004, founding chairman and CEO Chris Gladwin had a new idea. It came to him while musing about how to store his extensive collection of photos on his personal computer. There just wasn't enough storage on his computer to house all those pictures.

Storing those keepsakes online in the cloud might work, but Gladwin worried they might then, outside of his control, be subject to loss or perhaps hacking. Not surprising, since he's an MIT graduate, Gladwin began reading books on encryption, and a really big new idea came to him that could alter the way data (including his and others' pictures) were stored and secured.

He realized that the execution of his idea would require forming a high-tech company, putting together a team that could pull it off, and raising a lot of capital. While his MusicNow was a nice little company, a truly high-technology startup with this big of an idea had not been developed and funded in Chicago in many years. Such startups had been gravitating to places like Silicon Valley, the towns around Boston's Route 128, and the Washington DC metro area, so the decision to try to do all this in Chicago seemed on the surface to be potentially as risky a decision as going after the big idea in the first place.

Chicago, like many other cities, had once been a hub of bustling entrepreneurship, with many hard-driving, creative, fearless minds conjuring up the future. But such innovators—like Marshall Field in retailing, Potter Palmer in retailing and real estate, Michael Burke in telecommunications (Tellabs), the Galvin Family in electronics (Motorola), and Casey Cowell in data communications (U.S. Robotics)—seemed to be "yesterday's newspaper." Until Chris Gladwin came along, there had been a long dry spell, and never in the dot-com era had there been a high-tech company created in Chicago that brought to the Midwest's commercial capital that virtuous cycle of local entrepreneur, assembling local talent, and capitalized through local funding.

The creation of that virtuous cycle depended upon not just Gladwin's big idea and his ability to assemble the required talent, but also his ability to attract the necessary funding—first from friends and family, then from local venture capitalists, and then from the wider world of risk capital.

Fortunately, Chris Gladwin had a lot of friends. Even better, some of them were individual accredited investors.

Once he exhausted that source of funds (which happens even to friendly people with big ideas), he turned to professional high-tech venture capital investors. There were not many of these in Chicago, so it was a tough slog raising the additional $1 million he needed.

Fortunately for his new company, which he dubbed Cleversafe, Gladwin was (and still is) also a really decent, philanthropic sort. Practicing that philanthropic bent, Gladwin hosted a poker party with proceeds going to charity, to which he was able to attract several local entrepreneurs and venture capital investors.

One of the venture capital investors, Jim Dugan of OCA Ventures, knew Chris well and decided to back his idea, even though many other professional VC investors had already turned Gladwin down. Gladwin then went out on the road to find additional capital to join with Dugan and OCA, and ran into our then-actively investing firm, Batterson Venture Capital. Our firm, along with OCA, recognized that with the rise of big data, big data storage and security were soon to be a big deal.

"Fairy Tales Can Come True, It Can Happen to You … "

The rest, as they say, is history. It may have taken a bit longer than we expected, and ultimately $100 million in investments over time, but when Cleversafe was sold to IBM in late 2015 for $1.3 billion, there were an awful lot of smiling faces in Chicago; 80 millionaires were minted among friends, family, and Cleversafe employees, and numerous already accredited investors suddenly became a lot wealthier.

Gladwin's big idea and its intersection with practical need resulted in market demand, and brilliant execution resulted in a home run win for the entrepreneurial Gladwin, the company's employees, and its venture capital investors. Many got back more than 10 times their investment. The very earliest investors made a multiple of 40 times their early investment. Cleversafe proved that a major high-tech company could be created in Chicago in the 21st century, and so lots more are ready now to skip Silicon Valley and build their dream in the Midwestern heartland.

Opportunities like Cleversafe, while rare, are not unique. They are all around us, hoping for the risk funding—because venture capital is unquestionably risk capital—to enable them to turn their dreams into realities. This book will help you find them, understand them, and, with some pluck and luck, become a successful venture capital investor or VC-funded entrepreneur. The result could be personal wealth, job creation, and a capital contribution to our country. Simply stated, we hope this book will help you win!

Leonard A. Batterson
Kenneth M. Freeman
Chicago, Illinois

Introduction

Since the financial crisis of 2008–09, the American economy has struggled to grow at just 2%/year. Yes, there has been an extended stock bull market, but the bull must inevitably lose its vigor unless economic growth accelerates significantly.

With the stock market climbing sharply immediately following Donald Trump's election as our nation's 45th president, there are some betting that the Trump presidency will result in such an acceleration. We won't know whether such forecasts prove accurate, and to what degree, for some time. Stock market returns over the past seven or eight years admittedly look great, but that's due largely to the bounce-back in prices following the devastating collapse of 2008–09. A look at the stock market over a more extended time frame presents a more sobering picture. Factoring in all the ups and downs, from January 1, 2000 to January 1, 2017, the S&P 500 index grew just 2.7%/year. Add dividends paid by the S&P 500, which have averaged around 2% annually, and you're looking at an average annual return of slightly below 5% over that period.

Moreover, the rise in stock prices to historical highs has been helped in recent years by the near-zero interest rate environment, which has forced investors to turn disproportionately to stocks for any hope of decent returns. Therefore, even if economic growth accelerates, let's say to a 4% rate, the likely accompanying rise in interest rates to more normal levels should temper further prospective stock market gains.

Innovation: The Path to Wealth Creation and What Venture Capital Is All About

So how can the American Dream of wealth creation continue? The key is, and has always been, major innovation—new technology and new product development that address new needs or meet existing needs dramatically better.

The most successful major companies understand this. Today's Wall Street darlings—companies like Microsoft, Alphabet (the parent of Google), and Facebook—were yesterday's venture capital–funded startups. These companies understand that major innovation must never stop. Look at the publicized innovation efforts of Alphabet (now pursuing self-driving cars), Tesla owner Elon Musk (racing to commercialize space travel), and the major pharmaceutical and biotech firms creating new cures for diseases that won't go away.

Automotive companies such as Volvo and BMW have established formal venture capital arms. Even marketers of mundane food, household cleaning, and personal care products, such as Unilever, are setting up venture capital arms to fund innovative startups in their fields whose growth prospects they can then nurture with dollars, distribution clout, and management know-how.

So, a fair question from investors might be, why not just invest in the stocks of these big-league innovators? We'd never suggest that you not invest in these companies. They've demonstrated the ability over the years to grow their businesses and stockholder value. There is one caveat, though. Their already high share prices have baked in investor expectations of continued healthy growth. Hence, you may earn a respectable return on those stocks, but don't count on breakaway gains.

The biggest wealth creation opportunity—for both entrepreneurs and the investors who back them—is through market-changing innovation commercialized by new ventures. There are the latest winners, highly valued new ventures you've heard about—Uber, Airbnb, Instagram, Square, and many others. There are also the home runs that aren't household words. We just told you about one in the Preface that enriched many of our Batterson Venture Capital investors, a company called Cleversafe. Cleversafe's revolutionary innovations in data storage turned roughly $100 million in investments (to be clear, only about 4% from Batterson Venture Capital) into a $1.3 billion sale to IBM. And there are some doubles and triples out there, too, though the biggest money is to be made on the home runs.

As awareness of recent venture home runs has grown, there has been a surge in innovative venture activity. It's no longer limited to Silicon Valley and Boston's Route 128. Venture capital activity is flourishing in New York, Los Angeles, the DC metro area, Austin, and anywhere where creativity, ambition, and the funds to nurture it are found.

Venture incubators and supportive angels are emerging every-where. Cleversafe is a great example. While people often talk about the Midwest's conservatism and reliance on agriculture and heavy industry, Cleversafe's billion-dollar+ win was created in Chicago. In fact, *Inc.* recently reported that Chicago (which is where our funds are based) is now second behind only New York City in the number of fast growing private companies on the *Inc. 5000*.

The dollar growth in venture capital investment reflects this broadened activity. Venture capital investments in 2015 totaled $59 billion, up 153% since 2005. Importantly for our readers, for the past couple of years, investments by individuals have caught up with the dollars invested by the big institutions. The rich potential returns from venture capital used to be restricted to an exclusive club of institutions and the mega-wealthy, but are now becoming "democratized."

Venture capital returns historically have been handsome, averaging about 12%/year. That's a lot better than the almost 5% average return from the S&P 500 over the past 16 years, and almost anything beats today's near-zero interest rates.

Some venture capital leaders have done even better. The funds we've managed have generated investor returns averaging 28%/year over the past 30+ years. We've done that even through the dot-com collapse of 2000 and the broad economic plunge of 2008–09.

Our secret approach in fact isn't really a secret. We've shared it openly in the past, and will share it with you in this book. It takes lots of hard work, screening hundreds and even thousands of venture opportunities to select the few that we believe could grow into billion-dollar+ home runs. We review at least a hundred ventures for every one in which we invest. We usually get in early, while these ventures still carry low valuations, before others recognize their potential.

The exhaustive screening and due diligence pay great dividends. To be clear, we don't always get it right. But more than 35% of our investments have delivered some positive return to investors. While that might not sound so great, that's almost double the success rate of the industry in total. (It's like baseball, where a .350 batting average can win the batting title!) And our big winners like Cleversafe (and several others, including our multibillion-dollar exits for AOL and CyberSource) mean lots of new wealth for our investors.

Before we go further, though, let's be clear. Venture capital investment is not for the faint-hearted. It is a high-risk—and potentially high-reward—opportunity. Most new ventures fail. Just 10% of venture capital investments deliver the majority of all returns. In this book, we'll try to help you maximize your success odds *and* manage your risks. We don't believe that any investor should risk losing his or her proverbial shirt in venture capital.

It's a high-risk, high-reward potential situation for entrepreneurs, too. It's easier and lots less risky for talented, ambitious individuals to devote their talents to large, well-capitalized enterprises and make a comfortable living. But for the most ambitious individuals (and often the most talented), many of whom don't want to live under the yoke of corporate direction and are determined to do their own great thing, that is not enough. They seek the gold ring that can be captured only by building their own market-moving enterprise.

After they've started up by borrowing from credit cards and home equity lines and then tapping into supportive and hopefully well-heeled family and friends, they need to find the even-bigger funds to continue on. As startups succeed, their capital needs to realize their full potential grow sharply.

It's often said that venture successes inevitably take twice as long and require three times as many dollars as the entrepreneur expected. So he or she had better know what they're doing, and go after funds from the right sources—those who can provide the needed dollars today, as well as help in accessing the dollars they'll likely need later, along with the advice and professional help that may be even more critical to their ultimate success.

While this book was written to help both the investor and the entrepreneur learn what they need to know to succeed today, it should remain helpful for many years to come. Sure, like the economy and other markets in general, the venture capital playing field will change over time, just as it has always been changing and evolving. Nevertheless, the fundamentals will still apply.

Very simply, the venture capital marketplace exists to bring together: (1) investors willing to accept considerable risk in exchange for potential exceptional return on investment, and (2) entrepreneurs whose innovative developments are characterized by considerable uncertainty and risk as well as potential for outstanding wealth creation.

For anyone who thinks the greatest innovations are behind us and questions how much is still left to "invent," we say *thank you* for leaving the wealth opportunity from future innovations in the hands of those of us who can still dream and think big. Humankind's ever-increasing expectations and aspirations will inevitably motivate continued innovation. Add to that the needs resulting from natural resource constraints, climate change, and other environmental concerns, which we believe will drive even more innovation than we can imagine.

Here is a list of a dozen categories we believe will be huge opportunity areas for future innovation and new wealth creation, and we're betting there will be even more:

1. Advanced materials
2. Artificial intelligence
3. Big data and predictive analytics
4. Biological computers
5. Biomedical
6. The conquest of aging
7. The genome
8. Immunology
9. The Internet of Things and of Everything
10. Nanotechnology
11. Robotics
12. Virtual reality

Changes in the venture capital playing field will also contribute to making the coming years good ones for venture capital investors and great ones for entrepreneurs.

As we mentioned earlier, the accessibility of venture capital investment opportunities is becoming democratized. Today there are roughly a half million individual venture capital investors in the United States alone, and that number should expand dramatically in the coming years.

Recently launched online venture capital portals have opened investment access to America's estimated 10 million accredited investors (i.e., individuals and couples with net worth, excluding the value of their primary residence, of $1 million or more, as well as individuals with annual income of $200,000+ or couples with annual income of $300,000+). Further, the JOBS (Jumpstart Our Business Startups) Act allows venture capital firms to advertise to these accredited investors.

On top of that, regulations implementing Title III of the JOBS Act, enacted by the SEC in the spring of 2016, open venture capital investment access, albeit with tight limitations, to the rest of America, too. These JOBS Act provisions should increase substantially the availability of venture capital investment dollars. What a great time to be an aspiring entrepreneur!

Entrepreneurs will be helped further by advances in software and Internet technology already behind us, which have brought down the costs of initial startup requirements. Lower-cost startups are ideal for many online venture capital portals, even those restricted to accredited investors. These online portals typically set much lower minimum investment requirements than the more traditional firms, and so tend to invest fewer dollars in each of their deals. The new online portals open to non-accredited investors, which are further limited by the SEC as to how much they can invest in a single deal, are also particularly well suited to startups with lower early capital needs.

Ironically, more traditional venture capital firms like ours, which only allow investments from accredited investors and, even though accessible online, set a higher minimum investment requirement (our new firm, VCapital, has a minimum individual investment requirement of $25,000), welcome these new firms that are democratizing the industry. Frankly, they are so new relative to the typical lead time from investment to return that it's too soon to say how well they will do for investors (more on that later).

Nevertheless, for us, the ability of a venture to attract a large number of these firms' smaller investors represents valuable market intelligence, demonstrating early concept appeal. It's somewhat like virtual market research. If the venture goes on to show progress and has greater subsequent funding needs for expansion, we may be more likely to invest. We may not get in quite as early, but the risk when we do get in (which will likely still be early in the venture's growth) will probably be less, too—an acceptable tradeoff.

Notwithstanding possibly lower initial startup funding needs, most ventures with considerable potential will have increasing funding needs as they progress. In some cases, particularly in fields dealing with information technology, the importance of speed to market may require quite sizeable later-stage investments in order to accelerate expansion. In other fields, such as pharmaceuticals and biotechnology, later-stage FDA testing requirements carry extremely large costs. The risks even at these later stages are still inappropriate for banks or most alternative lenders, requiring a venture capitalist's perspective and risk tolerance.

Putting all this together, it looks like we are actually just now entering the golden age of venture capital for individual investors and the entrepreneurs whose dreams they will be able to fund and then benefit from financially. This book is written for both groups—individual investors and entrepreneurs—to help guide them along the path to potential wealth.

Building Wealth
through Venture Capital

PART

I

Understanding the Major Players

CHAPTER 1

The Venture Capitalist: Funder of Dreams

At the center of the venture capital playing field is the venture capitalist. The practical knowledge needed by both investors and aspiring entrepreneurs begins with a general understanding of this strange and extremely small population of individuals.

This chapter will get into a general description of our unique breed. Chapters 4 and 8 will then get into the distinguishing characteristics that investors and entrepreneurs, respectively, should consider in deciding which ones to invest with or to seek out for funding.

There are many ways to think about the venture capitalist. One is to liken him or her to a marriage broker. At its most basic level, the venture capitalist's reason for being is to bring together investors' dollars with entrepreneurs who need their money. Of course, the investor has to want to invest in that entrepreneur's venture, and the entrepreneur has to be willing to accept the investor's terms. The venture capitalist as marriage broker needs to sell both sides.

The venture capitalist is also like a marriage counselor. The "VC" helps the two sides—investors and entrepreneur—communicate with one another, often counseling the entrepreneur to enhance his or her venture's success odds. After all, the venture's continued progress and potential for ultimate success along with its attendant rewards are what will keep the relationship between investor and entrepreneur together.

Of course, one could describe the venture capitalist in other ways, too. The venture capitalist is part riverboat gambler, part security analyst, part trader, and part entrepreneurial voyeur.

3

Venture capital is a high-risk/high-potential-reward endeavor, so not surprisingly, venture capitalists are calculating gamblers, instinctively balancing the risks and rewards. No venture capitalist can win every time, but the successful ones' winners will handily compensate for the losers.

Successful venture capitalists have intuitive and analytical skills. They must be able to assemble and digest large amounts of data—some precise but some pretty vague and incomplete—and integrate all that information in order to make seriously consequential decisions.

The venture capitalist must be an astute trader and negotiator, the kind of talent Donald Trump would admire. To succeed, he must figure out what he can sell to whom (like deal potential, deal terms, and ultimately the successful venture he has funded and nurtured) and what he can buy from whom (professional services, shares of high-potential ventures) at a favorable price.

Even the successful venture capitalists, though, will lose more often than they win, so they must have confidence and strong egos. While recognizing that reality—that they'll lose more often than they win—they still must be able to state unequivocally that they believe in this entrepreneur and his or her venture, and to back that stated conviction with theirs and others' money.

The venture capitalist must often be a skeptic, as he is likely to reject a hundred deal opportunities for every one in which he invests funds. He also must temper the optimistic fervor of the entrepreneur. That's important at the start in order to negotiate a good deal and then later to foster the entrepreneur's management discipline and ensure the entrepreneur recognizes key risks and addresses them thoughtfully. At other times, he must be a business romantic, recognizing and accepting his limited control over the entrepreneur's operations and therefore often having to suspend lingering disbelief.

Venture capitalists must be extraordinary at living with and managing through ambiguity.

- Ambiguity in that not much can happen before he or she has investor money in hand, and often that money must be secured before he can even tell the investors the deals he has to offer.
- Ambiguity in that he or she must read between the lines, as investment decisions must be made before much of the information one would like is available.

- Ambiguity in that the investments are usually highly illiquid; most must be held for 5–10 years, through good times and bad, before success or failure can be known.
- Ambiguity in that entrepreneurs may love him as their essential source of money and yet hate him because of the controls and limitations he may insist on imposing in exchange for that money.
- Ambiguity in that investors must think enough of him to invest with him, may then grow impatient and displeased, waiting so many years for a return, and then love him dearly for the stellar returns he may ultimately deliver.

Venture capitalists must also have the confidence to live with frequent adversity. Almost all ventures in which he or she invests don't go quite as planned at the start. Most go through the valley of death at least once. Buckminster Fuller once wrote, "Sometimes I only find out where I should be going by going somewhere I don't want to be."

Most of all, the venture capitalist needs to be a business generalist. He or she is often required to provide not only know-how but also "know-*who*," to know the resources that the entrepreneur needs to best solve specific problems. Often the venture capitalist needs to know a lot about the particular industry, market, or technology in which he is investing his investors' funds.

Importantly, the venture capitalist must be highly knowledgeable about business development. That means sometimes being a patient nurturer of growth, but at other times being the impatient, sharp prod pushing the entrepreneur. Most people involved in business creation create just one business in a lifetime; the venture capitalist is involved in building many.

The venture capitalist must be an astute strategist. The ventures in which he invests are inevitably on the cutting edge of markets and technologies, so often those ventures need to make sharp strategic turns as more is learned. The successful venture capitalist must be able to participate in driving the venture's strategic path. Both investors and entrepreneurs need such VC skill.

Perhaps surprisingly, the successful venture capitalist must sometimes display exceptional operating acumen as well. While in most cases the venture capitalist will not get heavily involved in portfolio companies' day-to-day operations, there are times when the VC must step in, right an errant venture ship, and spearhead the turnaround of a venture that still has valuable potential but has lost its way.

There aren't many individuals who have all these tendencies and skills, and even fewer who want to live life on the edge like this. There are only about 500 active venture capital firms in America. Given all the aspiring entrepreneurs and ambitious startups vying for the support of so few VCs, the entrepreneur needs to understand the time pressures they face and the schedules they juggle. Don't lose faith if the call you made or the documents you sent don't receive responses for several days. The message you get that the VC is out of town or in meetings and can't get back to you right away is likely the truth, so don't despair.

CHAPTER 2

The Entrepreneur: His Mind and His "Cultivation"

Since our mission in writing this book is to provide practical how-to guidance for both investors and entrepreneurs seeking venture capital, it seems important early on to give both reader groups a better sense of what entrepreneurs are all about. Entrepreneurs need to understand some of the variables related to the probability of their success. Investors need to understand better what they should be looking for in entrepreneurs in whom they will entrust their support.

DNA of the Entrepreneur

The entrepreneurs we're talking about here are the ones doing the big new things that are the essence of the venture capital world. Our society, which more readily accepts a degree of conformity, has often made these "creators"—like prophets, persons of vision, and cutting-edge artists—march to their own distant drum. Their unique talent may be seen as a threat to those who are more conformist, less creative, and who do not always live by their wits. They are a real threat to the established (and the establishment), whether in art, business, science, or government. Their discoveries, inventions, and creations may well end the reign of the old if they prove to have greater utility and value.

Entrepreneurs are neither entirely alike nor entirely different. Nevertheless, we'll try to paint a general profile that captures a reasonable composite of the nature of those entrepreneurs who succeed in a big way.

7

Almost all are driven by their own particular demons to attempt to create their own unique destiny. They are generally uncomfortable with authority imposed by others. Many as children were unable to be true to themselves while attempting to conform and placate a concerned parent. Their characteristic hostility to authority, and the limitations they sense it imposes, is a response to these childhood chains.

The entrepreneur is not much interested in getting along by going along. They want to follow the beat of their own drum, and some see pursuing their target quickly, with urgency, as being necessary for survival. The best of the breed, though, while perhaps avoiding external authority and situations they feel they cannot control, do know their own limitations.

Driven by Passion

Entrepreneurs are driven by passion, often an all-consuming passion. There are no half measures on this field. If it doesn't work, try again. They are generally not in it for the money (although that would be nice), but instead for getting something out of themselves that they need to get out, for expressing themselves in their own special way. Bruce Springsteen says it well in his book, *Born to Run* (published in 2016 by Simon & Schuster), writing about his career journey: "I wanted something that could come only from my voice that was informed by the internal and external geography of my own experience." Bruce gets it exactly right; successful entrepreneurship is the external expression of a compelling inner need.

Entrepreneurship is both artistic drive and artistic expression. It reflects an *internal* drive that is converted into an *external* impact, resulting in product or company. Steve Jobs had an internal drive initially to create a desktop computer truly accessible to the masses. That resulted back in the early 1980s in the Apple II, which was at first sold mostly to schools and to parents with young kids. As someone driven by an especially powerful inner demon, though, Jobs couldn't stop there. His focused drive pivoted in different directions a number of times, leading to a worldwide brand of devices and their integrated software.

Springsteen and Jobs listened to their passions and followed the beat of their own distant drum, and that made all the difference.

Springsteen put it this way: "I wanted the singular creative and decision-making power of a solo artist, but I also wanted the live, rambunctious gang feeling that only a real rock-'n'-roll band can deliver. I felt there was no reason you couldn't have the best of both worlds, so I signed as a solo artist and hired my longtime neighborhood running pack as my band (the E-Street Band)."

Springsteen and Jobs both wanted it—insisted on it—their way, pursuing single-mindedly their vision, which guided subsequent direction and evolution. Their passion and drive gave them the power to pivot when times became tough, as is so often needed in a new entrepreneurial venture, as well as to bring others along with them. In Jobs' case, the almost-mystical persuasion of his "reality distortion field" led investors, employees, and ultimately consumers to believe almost anything he told them.

Motivated by the Opportunity to Make a Positive Difference

Often the best investments are those where the entrepreneur is way out on the leading edge of the possible. These breakout deals are generally priced right, with low early valuations/share price, and yet have the potential to disrupt or reinvent existing businesses and sometimes even entire industries.

These breakout developments represent potential opportunities for big profits while also often addressing a major problem or existing challenge to the health and welfare of our society. Solving big problems with disruptive innovation is the way to both riches and honor.

Northfield Laboratories, started just outside of Chicago in Northfield, Illinois, was such a company. In the mid-1980s, the AIDS epidemic was ravaging society, threatening to move into the mainstream as a serious pandemic. It needed to be contained. It was determined that one major source of transmission was blood transfusions. An "artificial blood" was needed that would be totally sterile and guaranteed free of AIDS or other bloodborne diseases, could be used for any patient without having to match blood types, and could be priced competitively to current blood transfusions.

About a decade earlier, unaware of the AIDS epidemic to come, a U.S. Navy doctor and surgeon in Vietnam saw many soldiers and sailors die on the battlefield because there was not such a product, particularly one that would not require matching blood types. Such a product would be invaluable for urgent battlefield emergency care.

When the doctor returned from the war, he was determined to create such a lifesaving blood product. He went to work, recruiting several researchers, funding product development through government and defense grants, and moving the development well along into animal trials. Then emergence of the AIDS crisis gave the project even greater urgency.

The nascent team came to this author's attention while I was a venture capital investor at the Allstate Insurance Company. At the time, Allstate's Venture Capital Division, which had been launched in 1958, was one of the oldest, largest, and most successful venture capital funds in the world. Its very first investment, both prescient and extraordinarily lucky, was an investment of $450,000 in Control Data Corporation. That investment serendipitously grew to nearly $50,000,000 in four years and hence "paid for all the losses ever after." With that financial backstop, along with continued support from Allstate senior management, the Allstate Venture Capital Division would on occasion roll the dice on potentially breakaway investments, particularly when there could also be a significant societal benefit. Northfield Laboratories was such an investment opportunity.

This author met with the Northfield team, and the company was quickly organized and funded, with Allstate as the lead investor, joined by Montgomery Medical Ventures, for which Allstate was also the lead venture fund investor. Almost immediately after this initial investment, another major Chicago company invested $40 million in the effort.

Several years later, even though the company's sought-after product was not yet ready for the market, Northfield went public at a high value. Still later, many investors realized substantial gains post-IPO, even as the company continued in R&D mode pursuing the sought-after artificial blood. Eventually over $200 million was invested in the technology.

The company *did* develop an artificial blood, called PolyHeme, a hemoglobin-based, oxygen-carrying blood substitute. Unfortunately, the product failed the final critical human trial by just two patients in Phase Three clinical testing, and so never received FDA approval, after an over-20-year attempt to create and commercialize lifesaving artificial blood. Had the clinical trial group been just slightly larger, the product might have passed the FDA hurdle, and there would be artificial blood available today.

The entrepreneur was out on the leading edge of the possible, and didn't get all the way there. In the case of Northfield Laboratories, though, money was made by the entrepreneur and his early investors, and a degree of honor secured, even though the product never made it to the market and to the patients whose lives depended on it.

The Need to Recognize Reality: Beware the Seduction of Money and Power

Most entrepreneurs are not driven principally by money or power, although both may result from their efforts. Most are driven primarily by a need for achievement and winning, and for the right to create based on their own unique vision.

Unfortunately, though, some entrepreneurs have been known to get themselves into trouble when they become seduced by early success and forget their animating vision. Trouble also can come when the vision becomes everything and is detached from reality. The recent tribulations of Elizabeth Holmes and her company, Theranos, are an instructive illustration.

From a very early age, Ms. Holmes envisioned a blood test that would require very little blood and avoid needles in the blood-gathering process. Modeling herself in part after Apple's Steve Jobs, including the all-black outfits, secrecy, board members of distinction, and eventually personal puff profiles in leading magazines such as *Vanity Fair*, Ms. Holmes seemed the embodiment of the Silicon Valley dream. After raising considerable venture capital (from only one major firm), her company became a mega-unicorn, privately valued at $9 billion.

It all came crashing down, however, when a *Wall Street Journal* reporter realized that the "Emperor" (or, in this case, Empress), while wearing Silicon Valley black, had inadequate technology clothes. Promotion got ahead of actual technology, disgruntled employees started talking out of school (one the grandson of a prominent member of Theranos' board), and the edifice began to crumble and its valuation to evaporate. Chances for any resurrection seem remote, especially since major distribution partner Walgreens has sued Theranos for fraudulent misrepresentation. A bold vision must be anchored firmly in the real world, with all important constituencies, including especially employees, positively aligned and on board for the ride.

A thoughtful postmortem (though the enterprise is not officially dead yet) suggests that Ms. Holmes possesses many of the traits and talents required of a successful entrepreneur. She clearly has demonstrated a high degree of personal commitment and dedication, and has pursued her dream with all-consuming intensity.

However, based on published reports, Theranos' communication was walled off into silos, and a need-to-know culture was created around the cult of the founder. Those silo walls were keeping employees out of the knowledge loop and thus unable to contribute optimally to addressing remaining challenges. Some entrepreneurs unfortunately reserve all interpretation of the vision and mission unto themselves alone, usually to their detriment.

For Theranos, the hard company pivot that is needed, along with Ms. Holmes' personal management transformation into a leader empowering her employees, is unlikely to ever have a real chance of happening. Hubris (a personality quality of extreme or foolish pride or dangerous overconfidence) and Nemesis (the Greek goddess who enacted retribution against those who succumb to hubris) were both present, much to Ms. Holmes' painful learning.

The Importance of Fortunate Timing

While passion and drive are essential to entrepreneurial success, timing also has to be right. Sometimes the right timing is nailed consciously, but sometimes it's really a matter of luck.

The reality is that a brilliant idea may fail because the entrepreneur's vision is simply too far ahead of his targeted market. Consider the case of Bill Von Meister, the founder of Control Video Corporation, a predecessor company to America Online (AOL).

Ironically, Bill Von Meister was related to the inventor and builder of the Hindenburg German passenger airship that caught fire at the end of one of its earliest voyages in 1937, killing 35 of the 97 people on board and bringing to an abrupt end the very brief era of airship travel. He may have inherited both his promotion and technical talent from his German relative, and maybe a penchant for poor timing, too, as the glory that was AOL ultimately accrued to his successor.

As for the American Von Meister, he got the idea in the early 1980s to download video games to the Atari video game machine over the phone line from computer banks located in Vienna, Virginia. Video games were then all the rage, and Von Meister, a telecommunications expert, had developed a 9600-baud modem that would connect the early home computer gaming users to bestselling video games on demand and that could be sold for $100. As Von Meister spun his story, eight major venture capital firms signed up and invested $12 million. The only problem was that, as one of the major VCs from Kleiner Perkins later said about sales of the device, "They could have shoplifted more off the back of a truck on California Route One than were sold." Von Meister had listened to his own internal distant drum and, while he was an effective pied piper to bigtime VC investors, he lacked the luck of timing. He came to the battle too early, concentrated all his forces in one big push, and lost the battle.

We discuss elsewhere in this book how Control Video Corporation managed to survive, to live another day and fight a new battle, this time very successfully. Led by a new management team that pivoted to a new strategic use of Von Meister's telecommunications technology advance, the ultimate result was America Online (AOL), the pioneer in bringing Internet connectivity to the home over common telephone lines. AOL went on to reach a peak market value at the time of its merger with Time Warner of over $350 billion!

Sometimes timing can be even more just pure luck. Peter Thiel and company, the team that started PayPal, recount that they raised critical funds to support the development of the company about a week before the Internet bubble burst in 2000. Lucky them! Meanwhile, our group at the original VCapital was about a week away from closing on an $18 million new funding with major investors when the bubble burst. Needless to say, the money didn't come our way. Thiel and his team became rich and famous, while we went back to work, having to create a new fund, raise new money, and find new deals.

We resurrected VCapital in 2016, when the online funding climate had once again shown its attraction to accredited investors, aided by passage of the JOBS Act, which permits fundraising media promotion among accredited investors (and now among non-accredited investors, too, albeit with strict dollar limits). Our team back in 2000 was just a week too late. Realistically, missing the open funding window by just a little, as we had, may not have been the worst thing. Given the market plunge and inhospitable investment climate after the bubble burst, even if we had raised the $18 million, that new money would have likely been lost anyway in the ventures we would have been investing in right away.

For those investing with VCapital (or other reputable venture capital firms) now, there's no reason to fret regarding the strength recently in U.S. public stock markets and the venture capital market. Experts do not see anything like an unsustainable bubble threatening to burst. The environment is very different today than in 2000. Today's market valuations are nothing like the run-up in share prices for almost every dot-com back in 2000.

Nevertheless, the lesson learned from Von Meister back in the early 1980s and from the dot-com bubble bursting in 2000 is clear. Timing can be an inescapable reality in venture capital fund raising and investing. Not going fast enough may cost a bundle in lost opportunity, yet delay may sometimes in fact save money.

Some would argue that we all create our own luck, and that luck comes the way of a prepared mind. It would be great if it were that simple, but it's not.

Most entrepreneurs with a realistic chance of raising major venture capital have a prepared mind ready to market their unique wares and often, though not always, a full business plan, a sparkling presentation deck, and a well-honed elevator pitch to capture immediate attention and interest. Most venture capital failures are not due to lack of preparation, but rather to the product or service failing to capture a sufficient market, even when it seemed to the VC investors as a high-potential opportunity. Lucky timing is essential, because once the product or service is ready for the market, the market must also be ready to embrace it. The supply and demand lines must intersect at just the right moment in time.

Von Meister of Control Video Corporation and, it could be argued, his famous ancestor, had the product, but the market was just not ready for it—neither for an airship that unfortunately crashed in what may have been a freak circumstance, or an online video game company that also crashed. Entrepreneurs who fail spectacularly like Von Meister and his ancestor often have trouble coming back, while others with luckier timing often reap the rewards.

Experience and Maturity Can Be Important, Too

Once ranked as the world's youngest self-made woman billionaire, with an estimated net worth of $4.5 billion based on Theranos' $9 billion valuation, Elizabeth Holmes' apparent downfall may have stemmed in part from her youth and corresponding lack of experience and maturity. Now 33 years old, Ms. Holmes founded Theranos when she was just 19.

Some of the successful entrepreneurs that venture capitalists support are admittedly just in their twenties, as were Bill Gates, Steve Jobs, and Mark Zuckerberg. These early years are the time when combined energy and new insight are at their peak potential.

Any younger, and experience and maturity will in most cases be insufficient, and credibility hard to achieve. Actually, most of the entrepreneurs that venture capitalists support are in their thirties and early forties. That is roughly the age-range sweet-spot when the combination of energy and new insight, along with maturity, experience, and resulting developed insight, are at their peak.

Many venture capitalists also prefer entrepreneurs who have gone through the valley of death with an unsuccessful venture at least once. A good combination can also be a young technical founder who is tuned into the latest and greatest technology, along with a CEO who has already been there and done that.

Recently our VCapital firm committed to invest in such a "May/December" founding team. That team consists of (1) a brilliant young tech founder with wide and deep expertise in machine learning, artificial intelligence, and predictive analytics, along with (2) an experienced CEO who has founded and successfully built a number of companies over many years and who also worked as a venture capitalist for a time.

Resolute, Energetic Drive Is the Most Common Denominator

Entrepreneurial success demands individuals with boundless energy, who have the natural drive to get out and get going—morning, afternoon, and evening. They are self-starters who never stop. They will call you on Saturdays, Sundays, holidays—at any time—with their ideas, questions, and plans. They are always working—planning their next move, examining the risks and opportunities in their decisions—and acting—always and ever acting. This is a restless bunch, rarely happy if not active and in motion.

The successful are both busy and focused. There is little purpose-less activity here; each step along the way is leading purposefully to somewhere meaningful. When the going gets tough, the successful entrepreneur gets tougher. Yet successful entrepreneurs can be tender on people during good times, even as they are consistently tough on results, but during lean times the successful are tough on both.

The entrepreneurial process requires faith and considerable courage. An entrepreneur often does not win the first time, as entrepreneurship is difficult to teach and hard to learn without going through considerable adversity. Winning the first time is often mostly luck, but it's resolute pluck that enables an entrepreneur to get up after a failure, dust himself off, and start all over again.

For the hardiest of the breed, bankruptcy—either company or personal—won't dampen their spirit. They will simply open a new shop down the street and continue business. The most intractable problems are likely to be viewed as a diversion on the road to winning and a worthy test of entrepreneurial mettle. The harder the challenge, the more opportunity for glory and gain. Being a successful entrepreneur is an undertaking for survivors, not necessarily for nice people, though of course some can be kind, compassionate, and genuinely nice as well.

They're Not Just Resolute; They Are Bold and Daring, Too

A calculated boldness is characteristic of most successful entrepreneurial ventures. This is the business world of the daring, of the strikingly unconventional, and even of the audacious.

High-technology entrepreneurs are often particularly bold in their conceptions and constructions. Their companies are working on the frontier, rejecting the window of the known and creatively disrupting and destructing what went before in creating a new future. This kind of work is larger-than-life activity, a deviation from normal, average human behavior.

Many times, the entrepreneur must step up with bet-the-company decisions. If events go even just slightly amiss, payrolls can be missed and the company gone. America Online and Cleversafe were in such precarious positions a number of times in their development. AOL went through a complete restage and restart, with the venture capitalists funding the company week-to-week, while a turnaround plan was put into place and early creditors and investors were calmed and brought back into the supportive fold.

Environments That Cultivate Entrepreneurs

For the past 60 to 70 years, Silicon Valley has been the number-one home of the brave and the bold. There have been, and remain, more venture capital funds in Silicon Valley than anywhere on the planet, and entrepreneurs have gone where the gold resides.

The Valley venture capital firms, particularly the early ones, were often started by either successful entrepreneurs and/or technologists or marketing and sales leaders who had a deep knowledge of a specific industry or domain of expertise. Being a highly networked business community, where just about everyone knew everyone else, helped both to raise initial funds (everyone knew who was bankable) as well as to facilitate startups, as an entrepreneur could pick up the phone and call others in the network who would provide the first, most important reference orders for the new company.

Once the Valley became the place to be, it became a magnet for aspiring entrepreneurs as well as a unique model for an effectively networked community, a major wealth-creating and job-creating engine. It was all built on silicon—grains of California sand and semiconductor silicon chips—and boundless human energy and innovation.

In recent years, the Silicon Valley innovation model has spread widely, as other geographical areas seek to emulate its wealth-creating engine. Steve Case, the marketing leader behind the rise of AOL, its CEO when it merged with Time Warner, and the author of the recent best seller, *The Third Wave,* calls this "The Rise of the Rest."

The presence of an environment designed to nurture the entrepreneurial growth engine is no longer limited to Silicon Valley or its early emulators, such as Route 128 around Boston, Seattle, Austin, and Washington, DC. Ambitious greenhouses cultivating entrepreneurial growth are emerging in New York, Chicago, Los Angeles, Cincinnati, St. Louis, Milwaukee, Detroit, Indianapolis, Philadelphia, San Diego, Phoenix, China, India, Costa Rica, and other venues around the world. Almost all are modeled after the Silicon Valley prototype, with each area taking advantage of its own unique resources, expertise, and pool of experienced talent.

Accelerators, incubators, seminars on how to be it and how to do it, university hubs, numerous courses, and so on, have sprung up even in the most remote, unlikely places.

The Emergence of an Entrepreneurial Ecosystem in Chicago

The Chicago area is a great illustration of the need for the right environment and what can happen when the entrepreneurial ecosystem is built. From 1871, the year of the great Chicago Fire, to today's 1871, the Chicago tech incubator housing hundreds of new startup companies, Chicago has been home to many entrepreneurs.

The early waves innovated in farm machinery (the McCormick Reaper), meatpacking, the railroads, real estate (Potter Palmer), and retailing (Marshall Field). Later, in the 20th century, as technology came to the fore, companies such as Motorola, Tellabs, and U.S. Robotics provided a hint of what was to come in technology development.

However, the Chicago-area universities were slow off the mark in creating a culture and infrastructure to foster high-tech entrepreneurship. The University of Chicago historically has been the home of a strong liberal arts tradition, and not so focused on science and technology, nor its twins, innovation and entrepreneurship. When one of the authors (Len Batterson) first came to Chicago in 1980, there were world-class technology and science ideas in the air, but zero culture or support from the major educational or governmental institutions for these nascent buds.

Being entrepreneurial by nature, this author and his brother Bill, then a PhD candidate at the University of Chicago, approached a number of top University of Chicago scientists whose work in the biomedical field showed promise of potentially rivaling Silicon Valley–based Genentech, whose recent IPO had met with acclaim. We worked with them to develop a business plan to launch a new company, named Helix.

Venture capitalists from other parts of the country expressed serious investment interest, but the Chicago VC community could not imagine a world-changing biotech company created in its own backyard. At the last minute, the University of Chicago scientists got cold feet about going ahead with the venture, as their colleagues at the University were aghast that members of the Ivory Tower would be seeking financial gain. Remarkably, one of the technologies under the tent of what would have become Helix was the expression of the gene for EPO, a compound that, when later synthesized at Columbia University, resulted in the key technology pillar of Amgen, the multibillion-dollar pharma/biotech company.

Chicago-area universities remained slow off the dime, taking about another ten years to create Arch Development Corporation, formed finally to spur commercialization of technology from the University of Chicago and Argonne National Laboratories, which was managed by the University of Chicago. Created with the encouragement and support of Allstate Venture Capital and others, the Arch Development Corporation facilitated the creation of a number of successful pioneering companies, including Nanophase Technologies, an early nanotech startup and IPO. Arch Development later morphed into the Arch Funds, one of the early Chicago-area VC firms to wander around university and other labs in search of the next big new things.

Before our local universities could build entrepreneurial momentum off of those early initiatives and really get in the game, Marc Andreessen at the University of Illinois created the first web browser. Not seeing the nurturing environment that has become so valuable in driving entrepreneurialism, Andreessen decamped to Silicon Valley to create Netscape and change the world—and for sure the Internet. Following the loss of two world-changing, multibillion-dollar market capitalization companies (i.e., Amgen and Netscape), and with Arch and a tech transfer park at Northwestern University finally up and running, the Midwest slowly woke up to the promise of high-tech entrepreneurship.

Since the entrepreneurially challenged days in Chicago, many flowers have bloomed. In addition to the tech incubator 1871, run by visionary Chicago entrepreneur Howard Tullman, which now houses over 400 digital startups, a second large tech incubator, called Matter, has also emerged. Housed in the Merchandise Mart (built by retail pioneer Marshall Field), it supports about 200 startups focused on life sciences and biomedical. The major universities now all have courses in entrepreneurship, business plan competitions, associated venture capital investment firms often funded by university alumni, tech accelerators, and mentor and coaching programs. VC funds have also emerged for minorities, women, military vets, and just about anyone with a good idea.

There is now substantial venture capital funding available in Chicago, and also coming in from both coasts and all around the country, as Chicago becomes more widely known as a center for tech and other innovation. Up until now, the startups spawned have been somewhat more modest, but Cleversafe, the first billion-dollar Chicago-founded tech company funded by Chicago-based individual investors and VCs, has moved this city into the big leagues. The 80+ millionaires minted through IBM's recent acquisition of Cleversafe are now reinvesting their gains in new Chicago-area startups—the virtuous cycle.

All it takes is for one venture to make it big like this in a city to change the culture and the startup ecosystem. When AOL's success created over 10,000 millionaires in the Washington, DC, area, that area became a major tech center for innovation and company creation. A similar entrepreneurial explosion happened in Israel when, funded by Athena SA, the first Israeli tech fund, an Israeli company was sold to AOL for a large gain.

The Age-Old Question: Nature or Nurture?

Lurking around the growth and development of the emerging worldwide entrepreneurial community is the elephant in the room. Is the capacity for successful entrepreneurship encoded in the DNA of an individual (or community), or can successful entrepreneurship be taught and developed anywhere among smart, motivated individuals? Just because a university offers dozens of classes in entrepreneurship, does that mean that its enrollees can really become the successful entrepreneurs the programs are designed to breed?

Without that fertile entrepreneurial support soil, it's difficult even for the hardiest of entrepreneurs, those with the most suitable DNA, to start a new company and achieve success. Many may try, but few will succeed really big. Encouragingly, the soil has become more fertile in numerous locales, with strengthening entrepreneurial ecosystems and more funding available.

Experiences in Chicago and elsewhere have shown that if the entrepreneurial drive is present, entrepreneurship can be taught, mentored, and learned. Of course, without the drive to win and achieve, heralded venture wins aren't likely to happen. In other words, the formula for entrepreneurial success increasingly looks like a combination of nature *and* nurture.

Having the innate passion and hunger to disrupt the status quo is essential. Then it's a matter of the vital entrepreneurial ecosystem as well as learning, perhaps through academia, but certainly by doing, whether or not one enjoys the benefits of university tutelage. If the fire is truly there, then the effort will be exciting, whether winning or losing. And then, as they say, if at first you don't succeed (because you probably won't the first time!), try, try again.

PART

II

For the Investor: A Guide to Realizing Big Returns

CHAPTER

3

Why Should *You* Invest in Venture Capital?

We love venture capital. For one of this book's authors (Len), it's been my life's work. For the other (Ken), it's been a later-in-life interest, as an investor and part-time strategic advisor, following a more traditional corporate executive career, and even while I continue as nonexecutive Chairman of a traditional, midsized manufacturing company (that makes candy and snack products, including chips that are edible rather than being made of silicon!). And for both authors, who now work together on VCapital, we are pleased to let you know that investing in venture capital has made lots of money for our investors, our partners, and for both authors' families.

But the question we need to answer here is, why should *you* invest in venture capital? While we've both made money at it, if anyone tries to sell you with promises of guaranteed wealth, don't believe him. As we'll remind you repeatedly, this is inherently a high-risk asset class. Nevertheless, there are sound, rational reasons for participating, even if you don't consider yourself a big risk-taker.

It Makes Sense Even for Conservative Investors

This is Ken speaking now. While Len's been at it for almost his entire career, let me tell you why I've been drawn to venture capital investment. You may find parallels in your own situation that make my thinking relevant to you.

I'd characterize myself as being pretty conservative, a "belt-and-suspenders type" is how one of my longtime friends put it. Both my wife and our longtime financial advisor agree. I'd characterize myself as a value investor. My interest in venture capital started after retiring from a career in Fortune 500–type companies. The retirement was fairly premature, as I was just in my mid-50s, when a serious heart attack scared me badly. Less than two months later, I was fired for the first time in my life because, as my boss put it, I couldn't run around the world as I'd been doing up until then.

That triggered my decision to leave my career and not even look for the next corporate senior executive opportunity. I'd done well, and didn't need to continue working to live comfortably. I hadn't quite reached that proverbial gold ring and won the CEO lottery, so we're not super-wealthy, but we're comfortable.

Incidentally, the heart attack and associated decision to leave the corporate treadmill were probably the best things that could have happened to me from a long-term health perspective. After focusing on cardiac rehabilitation, including a much healthier diet and daily exercise regime, 45 pounds were quickly shed, and less than five months post–heart attack my wife and I set off for a bike tour of Ireland, pedaling 30 miles a day. I subsequently caught the running bug, and wound up winning my town's annual 5K race (for my age class) and placing competitively in a number of larger races.

Getting back to the subject at hand, why did this conservative retiree decide to invest in venture capital? I'm the analytic and strategic type. Having a lot more time on my hands, and without more highly compensated work planned at the time, I began to think hard about how to manage our assets. I figured they needed to last another 30 or 40 years, at least for my wife and hopefully for me, too.

My reading on the subject kept bringing me back to the importance of asset allocation and the need for that asset allocation, notwithstanding my conservative personal nature, to include some portion invested in more aggressive growth vehicles. With the 2008–09 financial crisis upon us, the stock market plummeting, and interest rates heading rapidly toward zero, I recognized that long-term Treasury bills were certainly off the table and that I'd better find ways to hedge against a possible sharp run-up in inflation sometime in the future. Fortunately, as an accredited investor, I had more options open to me than most folks.

Before we go further into my thought process, let's first explain what it means to be an accredited investor. The SEC defines an accredited investor as: (1) an individual or couple with net worth, excluding their primary residence, of at least $1 million; or (2) an individual with an income of at least $200,000, or a couple with an income of at least $300,000, for the past two years and with a reasonable expectation of that continuing.

Being an accredited investor means you are well-off—not necessarily super-wealthy, but you do have some financial discretion. It also means that you're allowed to invest in asset classes like venture capital and other private securities that, until recently, non-accredited investors were not allowed to invest in. Recent regulatory developments from the SEC now allow individuals who have not attained accredited investor status to invest in venture capital as well, albeit in very limited amounts.

Serendipitously, unaware of my personal situation and resulting heightened interest in personal financial management, but simply having been a classmate at the Harvard Business School, Len Batterson reached out to me as a possible investor in Batterson Venture Capital. I'd honestly never before thought about venture capital. The background material he shared, though, was intriguing. The funds and investment teams he had led had a great track record.

Fortunately, my financial advisor is very bright, competent, and truly focused on his clients' financial well-being. When I asked him about investing in Batterson Venture Capital, even though his affiliation with a major brokerage firm precluded his benefiting at all from any such investment, he encouraged our jumping in.

He explained that venture capital doesn't have a tight correlation with the stock or bond markets. He viewed it as he would look at other alternative investments as well—as an asset class that over the long haul can help smooth out the ups and downs of the stock and bond markets, effectively reducing overall portfolio risk, despite the inherent riskiness of each individual venture capital investment. He explained that this benefit would be present as long as we took a reasonably diversified approach to this different asset class. In fact, when we began by investing a relatively modest amount, our advisor suggested we consider more in order to enable greater diversification, and we have indeed since increased our allocation.

To be clear, I'm not in venture capital to make a fortune. I realize you can't plan on that. In fact, reflecting my conservative bent, our initial investment was in Batterson Venture Capital's overall portfolio, not limited to just one or two ventures. That reduces risk, facilitating the diversification within this asset class just mentioned, while of course moderating potential gain as well. My motivation has been an opportunity to benefit from venture capital's overall historical 12% returns, and hoping for (but not counting on) my author partner's even better historical 28% return. Happily, some of my early investment dollars went into Cleversafe, which accounts for my frequent smile.

A Hedge Against Inflation and Lengthy Bear Markets

My original reason for thinking about including more aggressive growth vehicles in my overall asset allocation was a concern with potential future inflation. While inflation has been extremely tame in recent years, I remember well the hyperinflation of the late 1970s and early 1980s. Back then, prices were rising nearly 10% a year, mortgage rates reached 15% and higher, and if you didn't get double-digit raises every year, you were falling seriously behind.

Maybe that won't happen again in our lifetimes, but the near-zero interest rates over the past several years and never-ending government deficits scare me, as they could trigger a big inflation run-up. The experts are already warning that policies expected from the Trump administration, including substantial tax reductions and substantial infrastructure expenditures, are likely to keep government deficits high and drive at least some increase in the recent benign inflation rate. That's good reason to include at least some aggressive growth elements even in overall conservative financial plans for anyone who can afford the risk that more aggressive growth investments always entail.

And inflation is not the only worry. I also still remember vividly the sting of the broad collapse in both stock and bond prices in 2008–09. While my wife and I came out of all that okay, having avoided selling off much and instead largely staying the course with our portfolio, thanks again to our valued financial advisor, we recognize the potential for extreme volatility and big drops at the wrong time. This is a personal concern with my days of big corporate paychecks gone and our financial assets representing our main source of income.

Our 2008–09 market scare got me digging through historical data and uncovering some long stretches when the stock market—the place we've been taught to look to for reliable growth—either went down sharply or simply went nowhere positive for extended periods. You may be surprised. I was.

I looked at stock market levels at the start of 2000, the New Millennium, and then again at the start of 2017. Despite all we hear about extended bull markets, the S&P 500 index over that 17-year period grew at just 2.7% per year. Adding dividends averaging about 2% annually, someone investing broadly in the S&P 500 over that period likely realized an annual return rate of slightly below 5%. That's hardly the froth one might expect given all the talk about the bull market.

Then I remembered the economy's difficulties back when I was still in school in the early 1970s. Fortunately I wasn't in a position yet to worry about investing and building wealth, so the market's travails didn't mean much to me then. The historical data, though, sent a shiver down my spine. The S&P 500 index began a long-term drop at the start of 1973, and that index finally recovered back to its January 1973 level in 1983, and then dropped below that benchmark again later in 1983 and into 1984.

In a presentation Warren Buffett gave at a major investors' conference in 1999, at the height of the dot-com frenzy, his memory and historical digging proved even sharper than mine. As Alice Schroeder described so eloquently in her book, *The Snowball: Warren Buffett and the Business of Life* (published in 2008 by Bantam Books), Buffett reminded that audience, a savvy group made up of many of the country's most successful movers and shakers, about market risks, presciently warning about the likelihood of a precipitous market drop at some point, though he scrupulously avoided forecasting timing.

As recounted by Ms. Schroeder, Mr. Buffett's comments did highlight the timing risks of stock market investing. He explained, "In the short run, the market is a voting machine. In the long run, it's a weighing machine. Weight counts eventually. But votes count in the short term. Unfortunately, they have no literacy tests in terms of voting qualifications, as you've all learned." He then displayed on the conference room screen a simple PowerPoint slide.

Dow Jones Industrial Average	
December 31, 1964	874.12
December 31, 1981	875.00

He went on, "During these seventeen years, the size of the economy grew fivefold. The sales of the Fortune Five Hundred companies grew more than fivefold. Yet, during these seventeen years, the stock market went exactly nowhere."

Many of you reading this book may be old enough to remember what happened shortly after Buffett's 1999 presentation. The S&P 500 exited 1999 at 1469, but dropped to 880 by the end of 2002. The NASDAQ plunge was even worse. On March 10, 2000, that index peaked at an intra-day high of 5132. The index then declined to half its value within a year, and finally hit the bottom on October 10, 2002, with an intra-day low of 1108. While the index then gradually recovered, it did not trade for more than half of its peak value until May 2007, and it took until 2016 for the index to finally recover all the way to its March 2000 peak.

Too many investors "vote" repeatedly. They don't practice the buy-and-hold discipline espoused by Mr. Buffett. On an average day, 3–4 billion shares change hands in NYSE composite trading. Even worse, too many investors rush in following market run-ups and then sell in a panic as prices plunge. In the midst of some recent volatility, small investors have even lost small fortunes simply waiting minutes for trades to be executed. High-speed traders rely on split-second moves.

Venture capital investment, on the other hand, is far less susceptible to short-term price and valuation fickleness. It is long-term by nature, not intended for short-term trading, so you're unlikely to shoot yourself in the foot like you can do in the publicly traded securities markets. Its values are based more on a venture's long-term financial valuation rather than on short-term market vagaries.

Hedge Funds and Private Equity Buyout Funds No Longer So Attractive

By the way, if you think you can outfox the market by hitching your wagon to the hedge fund and activist investor icons, think twice. So much has been written about activist hedge funds and their wealthy leaders—like Carl Icahn, William Ackman, and Barry Rosenstein—that you may have assumed these guys were winning big and that investors in their funds could feel confident of big gains.

Some of the activist hedge funds were big winners years ago, hence their founders' personal fortunes. However, it looks like there may now be just too many dollars chasing not enough great ideas and so, of necessity when so many dollars flowed into their funds, some pretty questionable ideas received investment dollars, too. As a result, these funds are not doing so great these days. The *Wall Street Journal*, citing an index tracked by Hedge Fund Research, Inc., reported that the average activist hedge fund returned just an estimated 1.5% after fees during 2015, versus a 1.4% return for the S&P 500, and that 2015 was the third consecutive year of declining returns.

Here's a more surprising disappointment. Private equity funds aren't doing too well these days, either. Based on a white paper published by the Center for Economic and Policy Research, private equity funds' performance advantage relative to the S&P 500 has been shrinking in recent years. For background, the Center for Economic and Policy Research (www.cepr.net) is a Washington DC–based non-profit think tank focused on complex economic and social issues through professional research and public education.

The researchers found that the median PE buyout fund outper-formed the S&P 500 by 1.75 percentage points annually in the 1990s and by 1.5 percentage points in the early 2000s, but has performed only about the same as the S&P 500 since 2006. Moreover, the per-formance of PE buyout funds is worse when compared to a stock market index based on midcap companies more comparable to those found in private equity portfolios rather than one based on large-cap companies like the ones that make up the S&P 500.

Again, the problem has become too much money chasing after too few good deals. Per the previously cited white paper published by the Center for Economic and Policy Research, "By 2016, 4,100 private equity firms headquartered in the U.S. were competing against one another to acquire portfolio companies in an environ-ment in which the number of high-performing, undervalued target companies is shrinking. In addition to the $185 billion raised in 2015, buyout funds held another $460 billion in unspent funds—or 'dry powder'—from prior rounds of fundraising."

Venture Capital's Strong Historical Returns

That's enough bad news about the problems other asset classes are having. Let's focus again on the positives venture capital offers.

Importantly, venture capital is the lifeblood of major, fundamental innovation, the key to substantive economic growth. Think about the big business success stories of the past dozen years—Microsoft, Alphabet, Facebook, and so on. All were spawned by venture capital investment, and there are many more that have not yet gone public and are still operating on their own as well as ventures that were acquired by established companies that recognized and valued their growth potential. As a result, aggregate returns for the asset class have historically been outstanding, and there's no sign that will change anytime soon.

This is demonstrated well by the Thomson Reuters Venture Capital Research Index, launched in 2012 to replicate the venture capital industry as a whole. Based on that index, venture capital investment has on average returned 19.7% per year since 1996, notwithstanding the 2000 dot-com collapse, versus modest single-digit returns for traditional equities and bonds.

Don't Invest More Than You Can Afford to Lose

To be clear, neither of your authors is suggesting that you should invest a large share of your net worth in venture capital. It is inherently a high-risk/high-reward potential proposition. You shouldn't invest more in venture capital than you can afford to lose without meaningfully changing your life.

If you are an accredited investor, and most venture capital firms limit their investor rosters to accredited investors due to the strict restrictions in dealing with those who are not accredited investors, you should be able to risk, say, 5% of your net worth without potentially jeopardizing your financial health and future. If you're not an accredited investor, the SEC limits your venture capital investments anyway, precluding you from taking undue risks in this asset class.

Substantial Institutions Love Venture Capital

Getting back to the positive, *on average* returns are terrific. That's why most sophisticated pensions and endowments have come to the conclusion that allocating a portion of their total portfolio to venture capital (and other private equity investments, particularly when private equity funds were doing better) makes sense.

Yale University's endowment, often held up as a standard of investment excellence, has generated nearly a 30% average annual return on its venture capital and private equity investments since 1973. Their commitment is so great that the university has invested in a large satellite campus, west of Yale's hallowed downtown New Haven, Connecticut campus, dedicated largely to scientific and technological research, has actively fostered entrepreneurial development in its graduate business school, and has invested with thriving venture capital firms that have sprouted right in New Haven.

Again, keep in mind that institutions like Yale can diversify their venture capital allocation across a large number of promising ventures. While you won't be able to diversify your venture capital allocation to nearly the same degree, the high-risk/high-reward aspect of venture capital still makes diversification within this asset class important. However, you'll want to think about and implement a diversification strategy with your venture capital investment allocation that is quite different from the way you probably think about diversification in stocks and bonds. We'll come back to that issue later.

Emotional Reasons for Venture Capital Investment

You've heard the rational reasons for including venture capital investment in your asset allocation. Now let's discuss the more personal and emotional reasons, too.

Consider the personal satisfaction in helping enable ventures that deliver something for society that means a lot to you. Perhaps a loved one has suffered from the ravages of cancer, or Alzheimer's, or some other dread disease. Wouldn't it feel satisfying to invest in a venture that may bring a cure for, or better yet eradication of, the disease? Or maybe you feel passionate about saving the environment. Wouldn't it feel great to enable a venture that contributes importantly to your dreams of a greener world?

If you're fortunate enough to have your physical, security, and social needs met (thank you, Dr. Maslow, for your work in explaining the hierarchy of human needs), it's just natural to move on to wanting to help others and make a difference to the world. And having the opportunity for a potentially outstanding financial return at the same time would be great, too.

Still one more reason for investing in venture capital is that it can be exciting and fun. Investors in our funds have told us that, in a world of increasing gravitation to the plain-vanilla index funds, they look forward to hearing about the latest developments and growth achievements of the ventures they have funded. They tell us that the prospect of a 10-to-1 or 20-to-1 investment return is exciting.

And while we know that bragging isn't polite, wouldn't it be nice to regale your friends on the golf course or at cocktail parties with your off-the-charts investment finds?

CHAPTER

4

How to Find the Right Venture Capital Firm

Y ou've decided you want to invest in venture capital as one component of your overall asset allocation strategy. Now, how do you find which firm to invest with?

Surveying the Landscape of Venture Capital Firms

On the surface, there *appear* to be lots of options. According to FindTheCompany.com, there are around 1,200 venture capital firms to choose from. That includes some overseas firms as well as many that might be better characterized as angel groups.

While the line between venture capital firms and angel groups isn't always clear, other sources that use a tighter definition of venture capital firms estimate the number of U.S.-based venture capital firms in the 500–600 range. This excludes angel groups and individual angels, who generally invest even earlier in the evolution of a venture.

Unless you already know a lot about venture capital and also have a lot of time on your hands, we'd suggest you focus on venture capital firms and exclude angel groups from your consideration set. Angel groups generally require considerable time from their members, who typically handle the venture screening, due diligence, and investment administration tasks that are handled for you by professionals at more traditional venture capital firms.

Since this book attracted your attention, we're guessing you do not have extensive venture capital investment experience. If that's right, we'd strongly urge that you look for a firm with solid professional venture capital investment experience and practices. That will leave you with a smaller but still *apparently* robust number of choices. You'll be surprised to learn, though, that there really aren't as many firms to choose from as it may appear.

As you scan the venture capital horizon, you'll see that venture capital firms come in a broad range of sizes. Total capital held by these VC firms ranges from as little as $10–$20 million all the way to the billions. According to a list of U.S.-based venture capital firms compiled by WalkerSands Communications, a public relations firm focused on the high-tech venture and venture capital communities, the largest appears to be New Enterprise Associates in Menlo Park, California, with total capital reported at $11 billion. Next in line is Accel Partners in Palo Alto, California, with total capital reported at $8.8 billion. The WalkerSands list includes 53 firms with total capital of $1 billion+.

The practical reality is that you can scratch all those billion-dollar-plus firms off your list of possibilities, because they won't even take your money. Believe it or not, it can be difficult for individual investors to find seasoned, professionally managed venture capital firms that will let them in on the industry's historically strong returns.

Unless you're really wealthy, or extraordinarily well connected, or willing to invest a big portion of your net worth with a single VC firm, you shouldn't even consider the big firms. The minimum commitment for such firms could be in the *millions* of dollars. These firms' funds are generally limited to big institutional players like pension funds, college endowments, or a fund of funds.

Some of these leading firms may accept a commitment of *just* $1–$2 million, but unless your net worth is $10 million or more (in which case, congratulations!), we wouldn't recommend investing that much in venture capital. While we love venture capital—it has done very well for Len over the past 30+ years and for Ken over the past few years—we do not recommend investing more than 5% or so of your assets in it unless your assets are in at least that $10 million range or even greater. Since there are only about 1 million households in the United States with net worth of $5 million+ and less than half of those have a net worth of $10 million+, unless you're the proverbial needle in the haystack, even we wouldn't recommend committing $1–$2 million to this asset class, let alone trusting all that to just one fund.

You may have heard that some of these leading institutional firms have a smaller "sidecar fund" for individuals that they establish at the same time as their main fund. The bad news is that access to these specially created ancillary funds is very tight, usually just for the firm's major contacts, previous entrepreneurs, and other important business relationships. Unless you have those kinds of connections—and not many do—you can forget about these major firms.

Once you exclude those behemoths, as well as the do-it-yourself angel groups, you'll still need some way to segment the remaining number of choices in order to make your selection process manageable. There are a number of dimensions on which to segment the field. These include the *stage* in a venture's evolution when they most often invest, venture *industry*, and venture *geography*.

To dig through these variables, FindTheCompany.com has the most complete database we're aware of. Their summary list shows firm location, the venture/financing stages on which they focus, and the firm's minimum and maximum investments in any given deal. You can then drill down to a more substantial database at the firm level, showing numbers of deals they've done and the number of companies in their portfolio, specific portfolio companies and their industries, the size of each investment as well as cumulative funds invested, and the scale of their exits and the nature of each exit (e.g., IPO or acquisition). Notwithstanding the extensity of their database, though, it is not complete (nor do we suspect any is), as it doesn't even include our existing and new firms, despite a recent $1 billion+ exit for one of our portfolio companies that received considerable press.

Another helpful list can be found on the industry association's (National Venture Capital Association) website (www.nvca.org). Their website lists nearly 350 member firms and provides links to the website of each individual member firm. Again, this list is incomplete, including only member firms and so leaving out any (like our firms) that are not dues-paying members.

Let's look at some of the variables you can practically consider in selecting a firm with which to invest.

Firm Selection by Venture Stage Focus

Let's start with the stage in a venture's growth and maturation. Many venture capital firms focus their investments on just one or two venture stages. This strikes us as a good way to begin the sifting-to-selection process. Here is a description of the venture maturity and associated investment stages based on stage definitions in the 2015 National Venture Capital Association Yearbook.

Seed Stage

In this stage, a relatively small amount of capital is provided, usually to prove a marketplace/product concept. This stage usually involves market research and product development and then, assuming going-in hypotheses are borne out, beginning to build a management team and business plan. This is often before any actual marketing has taken place.

The funding for this stage, which typically comes after the entrepreneur has maxed out his or her credit cards and contributions from family and friends, is often sourced from individual angels and angel groups. However, it is also sometimes pursued by professionally managed venture capital firms, particularly firms that may be interested in investing in subsequent financing rounds if venture progress justifies that. This is what we meant when we said the line between venture capital firms and angel groups isn't always clear.

Financings at this stage are generally not more than about $500,000, and usually less, but could occasionally run up to the $1 million range. A presentation by the Angel Capital Association to the SEC in 2013 analyzing available 2012 private venture financings found angel/angel group investments averaging $342,000 per deal, this compared with an average venture capital financing round (across all venture stages) of $7.2 million.

Why would someone invest at such an early stage? Perhaps because it is the ultimate bargain; the venture's share price is inevitably lowest at this stage, so potential gain is greatest. But this stage is *really* not for the faint-hearted, as less is known about the venture so early in its development and so uncertainties are greatest at this initial stage.

Early Stage (Post-Seed)

Think about the process of venture maturation as being like a funnel. While lots of ambitious entrepreneurs set out to create the next Microsoft or Facebook, a large majority fall off the rails over time. The majority of the seed stage ventures will never even reach this post-seed early stage. Perhaps the hypotheses that motivated the venture will be invalidated, or it will appear likely to prospective investors (and maybe even to the founding entrepreneur) that success odds and return potential just aren't great enough to risk further investment.

For those ventures that pass this screening stage, their share prices will be higher than at the seed stage. Risks and uncertainties, while still great, will have diminished some. The probability of a positive return, while still pretty low, will be greater than before.

Financing needs at this stage are usually greater than at the seed stage, typically in the $0.5–$5 million range. This is where venture capital firms usually take over from the angels. At this stage, the venture generally is approaching product development completion and is focused on market testing or pilot production, with product refinement often still ongoing. While possibly still fleshing out its organizational structure, the company is often already selling in the marketplace on a limited scale.

This limited scale is usually too small to be profitable. While a venture might even be capable of operating profitably on such a limited scale, successful venture capital investors don't go after ventures for the limited profits associated with limited scale. Their objective is to invest in businesses with substantial growth potential that justifies continued aggressive investment, often to fund market testing in order to determine the optimal formula for eventual profit maximization. Continued enterprise losses at this stage usually are not a big concern. In addition, in some fields, such as in the medical area, where extensive testing and government approvals are required before any marketing can be done, the venture may still be far short of selling in the marketplace.

Expansion Stage

The winnowing down continues, and those ventures that reach what is called the expansion stage will have passed another critical stage gate. While ultimate marketplace success may still be uncertain, the odds are getting better. And the share price is usually increasing as well.

At this stage, the venture usually is being actively sold in the marketplace. The venture may already be profitable, but require substantial funds for rapidly growing receivables, inventories, and perhaps increased production capacity as well. Alternatively, the venture may still be operating at a loss while investing aggressively in envisioned substantial long-term growth. Risks are likely still great enough that a conventional lender like a bank is generally not viable.

The dollar magnitude of financing rounds continues to increase at this stage, typically to the $5–$25 million range. Some venture capital firms focus most of their dollars on this or even later financing stages. The larger the financing round, the more likely the money will come primarily from institutional investors and the less access individuals will have.

Firms still working primarily with individual investors may, however, participate as well at this stage, sometimes in support of ventures they funded earlier and that still hold attractive promise. (If the potential of a venture they funded earlier no longer seems as attractive, the firm's focus will instead be on recouping as much cash as they can—and that may be zero—limiting losses and moving on to greener pastures.)

Late Stage

At this point, the likelihood of marketplace sustainability is greater, even if ultimate growth potential is still uncertain. This is where the dollars sought for investment get really large, sometimes even in the hundreds of millions of dollars, as the business may need substantial investment capital for rapid growth and timely market domination.

At this stage, the venture may already be large and sometimes even well known, but its owners believe its value will be still greater as it more closely approaches longer term potential. Think about companies like Uber, Airbnb, and others that have already become household names but that still seek further investment to realize their full potential.

Share price is usually considerably higher at this point, as the risk of total failure and total loss is considerably less. Participation at this stage is generally limited to the major institutional venture capital firms catering primarily to institutional investors with the capacity to meet the much greater investment need.

Historically ventures had exited from the venture capital realm by this stage and pursued an *initial public offering* (IPO). However, in more recent times, given all the pressure public companies are under to report earnings progress quarter-after-quarter, some of these high potential ventures and their venture capital shareholders have chosen to remain private somewhat longer in their quest to minimize such pressures and focus on maximizing long-term gain. Of course, some of these *unicorns* (privately owned ventures valued at $1 billion+) may instead simply fear the reception they anticipate from the public market, which might result in a big fall in share value for its expansion- and late-stage venture capital investors.

Why Should You Care About a Firm's Venture Stage Focus?

So why should you care so much about the venture stage where a firm is focused? You might want to target your investment dollars at the seed or early stages, where there are fewer investors involved, because you want to have a personal influence on the direction of the company. Or perhaps you are inspired by the venture's mission, and hope your early investment not only makes you a healthy return but also makes a real difference to the world. Maybe you've lost a loved one to a particular disease and want to invest in a potential cure, and so you're ready to commit dollars as soon as there seems to be a reasonable opportunity. Or maybe you have always wanted to create a world-changing venture and see your investment dollars as a way to contribute to such a development.

From a financial standpoint, as we've discussed, investment at different stages carries different degrees of risk and associated potential gain. Quite simply, generally the earlier the venture/financing stage, the lower the share price, so the greater is the return potential, but the greater as well is the risk of total loss. (See Figure 4.1.)

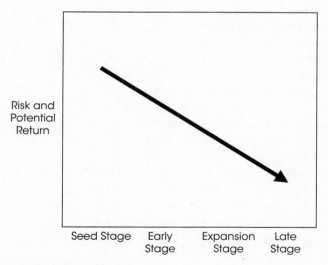

Figure 4.1   Risk/Reward Tradeoff by Stage

There are ways, though, of managing the greater risk of earlier-stage investment. One is through a firm's more insightful screening and rigorous vetting of its investment candidates in order to do a better job of deal selection. Another way is through your own investment diversification—just invest in more seed and/or early stage ventures to hedge your bets, as some percentage are likely to strike pay-dirt. We'll get more into thoughts on managing diversification later.

The firms Len has run have focused strategically on early stage investment, but generally not at the seed stage. While leaving seed investment to others may cause us to miss out on the very greatest return potential, it enables us to know more about the venture before investing. We thereby can better assess a venture's potential and success odds, leading to a higher batting average.

We believe one of our competitive strengths is rigorous deal screening and due diligence—superior deal selection—which requires the greater analytic opportunity that wouldn't be possible at the seed stage. While we do sometimes participate in later expansion-stage investments, when we believe strongly in a venture's potential and likelihood of success and also want to meet our investors' desire to increase their commitment, the higher share price as a venture matures also reduces the potential multiple we could ultimately realize on the investment.

Firm Selection by Industry Focus

Some venture capital firms differentiate themselves based on the industries in which they invest. They may invest in some predetermined range of strategic industries or perhaps even focus in just one or two. Some industries typically chosen for focus include information technology, telecommunications, mobile applications, big data, and biotechnology, to name just a few—industries where there's lots of market-changing innovation.

Some investors select a venture capital firm based on its focal industries. Perhaps an individual believes strongly in the growth potential of certain industries and therefore wants to focus her venture capital dollars in those industries. Or perhaps an individual is particularly knowledgeable about an industry. That person might then have a greater interest as well as possibly better ability to select specific venture capital deals in that industry. Or an individual may choose to invest based on some personal mission. A person who lost a loved one to cancer might be motivated to invest with venture capital firms focused on biomedical ventures and go on from there to invest specifically in their deals focused on cancer treatment.

While most venture capital firms tend to focus on high tech, regardless of the specific industry or technology, that's not the case for all. For instance, there are firms that invest specifically in consumer products, services, and retailing ventures.

One of our most illustrious business school classmates, Tom Stemberg, who earlier in his career founded office super store pioneer Staples, spent the final years of his career, before his tragic, untimely death, heading up a venture capital firm focused specifically on consumer products, services, and retailing ventures. While some of those ventures have admittedly been highly innovative and strategically astute, most have also been far from high tech. If you're a consumer products heavyweight, you might choose to invest with such a firm to take advantage of your experience, knowledge, and interest.

As Len has done with his previous funds, our current firm, VCapital, is focused on high tech and hard science. Specific industry sectors include mobile digital products and services, cloud computing and big data, media and telecom, biotechnology, medical devices, and biomedical and drug discovery. These broad sectors have the potential to produce and capitalize on disruptive technologies, reach a large and addressable market, and provide significant commercial opportunities.

These are also sectors our team knows and understands. They are consistent with Len's previous funds, which invested in and influenced such winners as America Online (known more broadly now as AOL), Atlantic America Cablevision, Illinois Superconductor (now called ISCO International), Nanophase Technologies Corporation, CyberSource, and Cleversafe. For younger readers, AOL was the pioneer in bringing Internet connectivity into people's homes. As discussed earlier, Cleversafe, which has pioneered tremendous innovation in data storage, is the only company on this brief list that did not exit via IPO; it was instead acquired by IBM in late 2015 for over $1 billion. AOL and CyberSource also grew into enterprises valued at over $1 billion. In fact, at its peak, AOL was valued at $364 billion.

As you consider venture capital firm options, keep in mind that they are *not* one-person operations. Our VCapital team includes seasoned executives from industry sectors we focus on, to guide in our assessment of ventures in our targeted industries.

Firm Selection Based on Geographic Focus

Some firms focus their investment activity in particular geographic regions. That's not as surprising as it might sound. Venture capital management is a labor-intensive endeavor. A VC may review hundreds of deal opportunities in order to find a small number to really zero in on for the most rigorous vetting. Vetting those finalists may require extensive observation of their operations and management teams. There's sometimes no substitute for onsite observation in such analysis. Geographic proximity makes that much easier and more efficient.

Similarly, once the venture capital firm has pulled the trigger and invested, its principals will want to remain in close contact with the venture management team. That's needed to keep informed, to provide consultative help, and in some cases to intervene in order to protect the firm's investment. Geographic proximity can help make all that more manageable.

Many venture capital firms focus on popular hotbeds of high-tech innovation. Silicon Valley (i.e., the San Francisco and San Jose metro areas) is at the top of that list. Other hotspots include the Route 128 circle around Boston and the Austin, Texas metro area. These areas benefit from a professional infrastructure that encourages and supports startups. However, they also can foster an investor frenzy, with too many dollars chasing available deals, resulting in early share prices too high for many investors' liking.

Len's firms' geographic focus through most of his career, including currently with VCapital, has been the Midwest, far away from the Silicon Valley herd, with Chicago as its bullseye. We won't pass up great deals from other regions, including Silicon Valley, but we believe the Midwest represents exceptional opportunity.

The region's outstanding universities and diverse industries create a wealth of intellectual capital—the seeds of venture capital. Yet the region's history and culture mean less investor competition for the best deals, resulting in better deal values and therefore superior investor return potential. Moreover, the extensive and diverse industrial environment can facilitate venture exits through corporate acquisition rather than having to wait for an IPO, which can mean more reliable and timely return on venture capital investment. This thinking is captured graphically in Figure 4.2.

Midwest as % of U.S.:

GDP — 19%

Patents — 19%

Computer Science Degrees — 25%

Fortune 500 Headquarters — 30%

Venture Capital Investment $'s — 5%

Figure 4.2   Why the Midwest?
Sources: Forbes; DriveCapital.com

Len's team's track record speaks to the wisdom of this Midwest focus. Most of our big winners have been Midwest-based. Our latest home run, Cleversafe, is Chicago-based, as is our VCapital firm. Nanophase Technologies and ISCO International are also Illinois-based.

The Chicago metro area in particular is the go-to destination for the region's top university graduates and entrepreneurs. Latest venture capital results from this third largest city in America are impressive—2015 startup funding of $1.7 billion and about 40 exits generating $8.2 billion for their investors. In fact, according to data from PitchBook, a Seattle-based research firm, over the past ten years, among ventures that have exited, 45% of Chicago-based venture deals that raised at least $500k produced returns of more than 10-fold, a greater rate of home runs than any other U.S. city, and 81% of Chicago exits generated investor returns of at least 3×, again higher than any other U.S. city. (*Source:* John Pletz, *Crain's Chicago Business.*)

The New Online Equity Crowdfunders

You may have heard of and be wondering about the new online equity crowdfunding firms, such as FundersClub, CircleUp, Seed-Invest, or AngelList, to name just a few. They may seem ideal to novice venture capital investors due to their low minimum investment requirements—often just $3,000–$5,000 and sometimes even as low as $1,000.

We urge caution. The backgrounds of the management of some of these firms appear to be more in information technology than in venture capital, and these firms are so new that the jury is still out on their investment acumen. Most VC-funded ventures take 5–10 years to exit, so it's just too early to assess their investment results.

We hesitate to denigrate the competition. We VCs do try to operate as a symbiotic ecosystem, frequently partnering with other firms in investment syndicates to best meet the needs of investors and entrepreneurs. However, when we look at all the resources some of these equity crowdfunders have devoted to fundraising and to their website technology platforms, they seem more like Internet plays than professional venture capital firms.

Our concern with these new online equity crowdfunders is compounded by their vast portfolios of deals. They typically offer dozens and sometimes even 100 or more deals. They look almost like venture capital flea markets. While they surely practice some analytical rigor in their deal selection, we don't see how they can screen and vet all those investment options with nearly the rigor practiced by more traditional professional venture capitalists.

Admittedly, as members of a seasoned, professional venture capital firm, we're biased. Conceding that bias, let's come back to what should be our readers' highest priority need—seasoned, professional investment management to maximize the likelihood of the robust returns that attracted you to considering venture capital in the first place.

Again, it's too soon to know if the new equity crowdfunders will measure up on that criterion. Our guess is that the best these firms, with their extensive portfolios, will be able to achieve is to come close to delivering industry-average returns. We'd even venture (no pun intended) a step further and forecast that these crowdfunders will do less well than the industry averages, because we don't see how they can perform as well as the universe of professionally managed, more discriminating firms.

While our new firm, VCapital, offers an online investment portal as well, it is not a crowdfunding site like these just-mentioned firms.

Our technology platform has been kept pretty simple and straightforward and our fundraising resources pretty basic. We offer an online investment portal because today's individual investors expect and demand its accessibility, convenience, and transparency.

Our $25,000 minimum investment requirement, though, means we don't need thousands of investors like the crowdfunders. We therefore don't need the technology and fundraising resources required by the crowdfunders. Our target is more discerning individual accredited investors. Our resources can therefore be devoted more to professional investment management and subsequent engagement with our portfolio ventures, to best address our investors' primary objective, outstanding returns. While VCapital, too, is a new firm, its team has a long track record with its predecessor firms. Our professional investment management bona fides are proven.

To be clear, we are not alone. There are other highly qualified, professionally managed venture capital firms as well. Our point is that these are the sorts of firms we'd recommend that you look for.

Other Resources for Selecting a Venture Capital Firm

In addition to the largely do-it-yourself online approach discussed thus far, another good source for finding the right venture capital firm for you might be through recommendations from relevant experts. These might include:

- Attorneys, especially those involved in VC/entrepreneur deal-making
- Accountants, particularly those with clients who are substantial investors or those involved extensively with businesses in their startup or early stage
- Entrepreneurs who have ever secured, sought out, or considered seeking venture capital funding

Regardless of what side of the relationship these experts may have been on—for example, attorneys representing either the VC or the entrepreneur seeking funding—their exposure should give them some feel for which firms might suit your investment needs and preferences and your investor personality.

Vetting Venture Capital Firm Candidates

You've narrowed down your search to a short list of venture capital firm candidates with whom you are considering entrusting your hard-earned investment dollars. How do you further assess those candidates and make a choice?

We'd suggest you first go to the firms' websites. Consider what you see. You'll get a sense for the way they think about their mission and about investing *your* money. You'll see where they focus from an industry standpoint. You'll likely see what's in their existing portfolio and probably hear about their successes.

Hopefully the websites will give you a feel for each candidate firm's team. Is the team filled with marketing and IT-type people? That could be a warning sign, suggesting they are focused even more on raising money than on investing most wisely for you. Or do you see a heavy dose of investment professionals and experts who are dedicated to making the best investment selections and who could then help the firm's portfolio companies?

There are often photos that at least suggest something about key people's demographics. Do the team members look really young, so they may know technology well but may be less likely to have the investing and consulting experience that could be vital? Or do you see team member maturity that will more likely have the business and investment experience that may be more important? Photo settings and attire may also tell you a little about the firm's personality. Are they conveying any particular image that may be relevant to understanding their approach?

The resources included on their websites, such as blog posts, podcasts, or links to articles, may tell you something about what's important to the key people on the team. Are they stressing investor education (maybe a good fit for a novice venture capital investor)? Or might they be stressing their vision regarding future marketplace trends and anticipated investment opportunities (also maybe a positive sign)?

Unfortunately, what you won't find on some firms' websites is any *clear* articulation of how well they've done. They may talk about some big exits. The website FindTheCompany.com actually does an extensive job of detailing how much has been invested and even showing the scale of exits since 2003.

But it's tough to find the kinds of numbers you'd really like to see, especially a firm's *realized* average annual return or internal rate of return for an extended period (i.e., the returns they've actually delivered based on deal exits). You may see numbers touting tremendous growth in the value of their investments. Keep in mind, though, that these valuations mean little until there's an exit and you collect your share of the cash.

Given the long-term nature of venture capital investments, securing *realized* returns data for existing funds is understandably difficult. The next best data is the realized returns the firm or investment team has delivered through its previous funds. Notwithstanding the disclaimer, "Past results are no guarantee of future performance," which you so often hear from financial services firms, that past performance may indeed be the best indication you can get of future results in this industry.

Those hard historical measures may sometimes be difficult to get ahold of. In fairness to other VCs, some are concerned with the legal and regulatory risks around communicating such hard numbers. They may fear that such communication can leave them open to legal issues should others not agree, for example, with their methodology for calculating those numbers.

We have faced that same challenge in presenting our team's new firm, VCapital, though we have decided that such performance track record reporting is too important to leave out. We have therefore gone to great lengths to detail historical results deal-by-deal, showing the losers as well as the winners, to ensure supportability and credibility.

Many firms are reluctant to disclose all those details, especially because of the industry's typical 80–85% deal failure rate. Hence, you may need to communicate privately with your venture capital firm candidates and probe aggressively for such hard numbers. They may share with you privately data details that they do not feel comfortable promoting publicly.

If you do that, don't let them fool you with measures that include current valuations for ventures that have not yet exited. Some of our more marketing-aggressive fraternity may try to sell you with such measures. For example, anyone who invested in Uber some time ago might want to include in their calculations the current value of that earlier investment based on Uber's latest $66 billion valuation.

But until an exit actually happens, or the firm in question has already sold its shares, that $66 billion valuation doesn't mean too much. It could still be driven down by many factors, for example, more market retreats like in China, where Uber recently withdrew; more municipalities that either push Uber out or simply bestow greater advantages on their licensed cab fleets, as is happening right now in London; or adverse legal rulings regarding the relationship between Uber and its drivers that could significantly change the company's economic model. So be sure you know what the numbers they show you really mean.

5

Venture Capital Investment versus "Buffett's Real Rules" of Investment

Earlier in this book, we told you that, over the long haul, returns on venture capital investment industry-wide have averaged about 12%. We also mentioned that more recently, over roughly the past 20 years, the venture capital industry average return has been an even more robust 19.7%, according to the Thomson Reuters Venture Capital Research Index, which is designed to replicate the venture capital industry as a whole. We're not aware of any such scientific index available earlier, so the longer-term rough estimate is just that, an informal estimate.

We also shared with you long-term returns for the S&P 500, which averaged slightly below 5% annually for the period from January 1, 2000 to January 1, 2017. To keep the playing field as fairly balanced as possible, just as we cited the more recent, more robust venture capital returns, we looked for a different time period that would result in better S&P 500 returns. We found that over a longer, 30-year period (which included the more-bullish late 1980s and 1990s), the S&P 500 returned an average of 9.9%/year.

While the venture capital returns still look better, one would expect that comparison given venture capital's greater inherent riskiness. The 9.9% return rate for the S&P 500 looks pretty good as well. So, why not just stick with the S&P 500 for the really long haul and not try to outsmart the market?

That's all well and good if that's really what you do. While the specific timing of your investments and ultimate withdrawals could either help or hurt you, chances are you'll come out okay. However, the reality is that the average investor does try to outsmart the market, and moves in and out of stocks inefficiently, too often buying high and selling low and incurring all those trading charges along the way.

But let's assume you're smarter than the average individual investor. You're not one of those impatient types who follow the herd, buying too often when things are high and then selling when they're low. We'll further assume that, since you're investing your time to read this book, you've studied other aspects of the market as well. We therefore assume you know that a recognized gold standard in investment expertise is Warren Buffett, and perhaps you've committed to following Buffett's rules of investment.

We share your admiration for Warren Buffett. He has achieved annualized returns for his investors over the past 50+ years averaging above 20%. While we've told you that Len's firms' venture capital investments have achieved returns over 30+ years averaging 28%/year, neither of us claims to be nearly as smart as Warren Buffett.

Let's look at "Buffett's Real Rules" and then compare how Len's venture capital investment approach compares to those principles. You'll see that they are surprisingly similar. The reason Len has been able to beat the Oracle of Omaha reflects the very nature of venture capital investment versus Buffett's traditional stock market investing. Let's explore both and compare.

"Buffett's Real Rules"

This compilation of Buffett's investment principles synthesizes observations from a number of sources, most notably Alice Schroeder's *The Snowball: Warren Buffett and the Business of Life* (probably the most comprehensive biography written on Buffett), *Business Insider*, and even *AARP The Magazine*. (They have some very thoughtful financial pieces given the strong interest of many 50+ readers.) Because this is a synthesis, the words won't match these sources' exact articulations, but we're comfortable that the essence has been faithfully retained.

1. *Buy at low-to-fair prices. Don't overpay.*

Buffett has always sought out attractive intrinsic value that exceeds the price paid. As he and his key long-term partner, Charlie Munger, have pointed out repeatedly, price and value are not the same. "Price is what you pay; value is what you get" (*Letter to Berkshire Hathaway shareholders, 2008*).

Buffett also cautions not to be fooled by "that Cinderella feeling" you get from what appear to be great returns due simply to irrationally inflated valuations. "Continuing to speculate in companies that have gigantic valuations relative to the cash they are likely to generate in the future will likely bring on pumpkins and mice" (*Letter to Berkshire Hathaway shareholders, 2000*).

His early gains were due largely to his ability to see intrinsic value where others did not. That sometimes included simply recognizing the value of a company's cash and other liquid asset holdings. As his wealth grew, that recognition focused increasingly on recognizing the substantial cash flows that could be generated by companies he acquired in such unglamorous categories as insurance and railroads.

2. *Invest in companies with vigilant leadership.*

Buffett has always placed tremendous importance on the investment target company's senior-most leadership, their detailed understanding of their business, and their focus on risk management and control. He believes in investing in companies whose cash generation "can be reinvested by good management in a business they know and which has a unique position" (*Business Insider*).

3. *Invest in business you understand.*

Some might even articulate this principle, at least in Buffett's mind, as to "embrace the boring" (*AARP The Magazine*). Buffett sees risk in part as pursuing business you don't understand. This is why historically he has avoided the tech sector, which he admits to not understanding, though some of Buffett's younger lieutenants are now channeling his Berkshire Hathaway dollars into the tech sector as well.

4. *Invest in companies with solid long-term prospects. Buy and hold.*

Buffett looks for companies with consistent, positively trending earnings over at least the past ten years, and suggests that a 30-year horizon be your window to the future. He has therefore avoided explicitly since the 1990s businesses that he feels are likely to be impacted substantively by the Internet, given his self-professed lack of understanding.

5. *Don't shy away from revolutionary investments. Just be sure you understand them.*

According to Bloomberg, Buffett has $15 billion invested in solar and wind energy. He may have avoided tech stocks, at least until recently, due to a lack of understanding of that sector, but where he can understand the market and its basis for interest, and he has faith in the management, he is willing to commit to his and the management's vision.

This was the thinking behind Berkshire Hathaway's 2008 investment in GE. In explaining that investment, Mr. Buffett expressed confidence in GE's strong management leadership and brand equity in the renewable energy industry, and especially in wind energy and the turbine business. Those are businesses where Buffett's financial acumen enables clear understanding of the fundamentals of heavy capital investment followed by a likely long stream of predictable operating cash flow.

6. *Look for companies with top brands and the ability to "control" prices.*

He understands that brands have greater value than "just selling stuff." "It's far better to buy a wonderful company at a fair price than a fair company at a wonderful price" (*Letter to Berkshire Hathaway shareholders, 1989*). American Express, Coca-Cola, and Wrigley are three companies whose shares he has bought aggressively due to the strength of their iconic brands.

7. *Always be liquid. Have a source of low-cost money ready to invest.*

This is why Buffett early on focused so much on insurance companies and banks. They provided a ready source of investment cash so he had the flexibility to pounce on good opportunities and did not need to rely on leverage through debt, which he has always hated. He "pledged to always run Berkshire with more than ample cash.... When forced to choose, I will not trade even a night's sleep for the chance of extra profits" (*Letter to Berkshire Hathaway shareholders, 2008*). This is why a related principle for Buffett was never to pay a dividend.

8. *Be very selective. You don't have to move on every opportunity.*

"The stock market is a no-called-strike game. You don't have to swing at everything—you can wait for your pitch" (*The Tao of Warren Buffett* via *Business Insider*).

9. *Keep doing the above in good times and in bad.*

"We've usually made our best purchases when apprehensions about some macro event were at their peak. Fear is the foe of the faddist, but the friend of the fundamentalist" (*Letter to Berkshire Hathaway shareholders, 1994*).

10. *Minimize your mistakes, and learn from the ones you make.*

Earlier, when he had far lesser reserves, Buffett was more risk averse and more focused on being sure he could sell what turned out to be a bad deal at a fair price to avoid (or at least minimize) losses. His mantra during those earlier days was, "Rule No. 1: Never lose money. Rule No. 2: Don't forget Rule No. 1" (*The Tao of Warren Buffett* via *Business Insider*).

How Len's Venture Capital Investment Principles Are Similar

You're probably wondering now how the venture capital investment principles Len and his team have learned and followed over the years could be similar to "Buffett's Real Rules." After all, the Oracle of Omaha buys insurance companies, railroads, soda pop, and chewing gum while Len's team pursues categories, like the digital tech sector and biotechnology, that Buffett historically has avoided. Let's go back through Buffett's rules one at a time and compare.

1. *Buy at low-to-fair prices. Don't overpay.*

While we stated earlier that in the case of the biggest home runs, like AOL, the initial investment price paid doesn't matter much, there aren't many AOLs. The singles and doubles are greater in number, and for them the price paid does matter. Also, even most investment home runs aren't the tape-measure grand-slams that AOL was, so price paid can matter at least somewhat. Moreover, for all the deals that don't succeed, the prices paid can help moderate the inevitable losses.

Importantly as well, Len's team has always avoided the "Cinderellas," those ventures that have already been bid up in price to what we consider excessive levels. The best examples are the unicorns. Who knows, maybe Uber will eventually generate the cash flows justifying its current $66 billion valuation and beyond, but we both believe that's way too risky. That would require virtually everything to go right for them. We wouldn't bet on that, and we don't want our investors to feel like they've bought "pumpkins and mice," to continue the Cinderella analogy.

2. *Invest in companies with vigilant leadership.*

We couldn't agree more with Mr. Buffett on this one. Our team places huge importance on a venture's management, its ownership commitment, and its operating capabilities. Vision and technology alone are not enough. Even the early stage companies we invest in need operating skill, disciplined execution, and financial control. The jockey can be just as important as the horse!

3. *Invest in business you understand.*

Again we are on the same page. Len's teams over the years have always focused on high tech and hard science—in industries including digital products and services, cloud computing and big data, media and telecom, and biomedical and drug discovery—because those are sectors the team understands. It's great that they are broad sectors with the potential to produce and capitalize on disruptive technologies, reach a large and addressable market, and provide significant commercial opportunities, but it's equally essential that the team understands them so it can assess the opportunities more knowledgeably. Our VCapital team includes seasoned executives from industry sectors we focus on.

4. *Invest in companies with solid long-term prospects. Buy and hold.*

This is at the core of venture capital. We invest for the long-term. We're not looking for short-term trading opportunities or flipping positions simply because valuations rise. We may not plan on Buffett's 20- or 30-year horizons, and we admittedly invest with the aim of an exit within a reasonable timeframe. But those timeframes are generally 5 to 10 years—sometimes shorter, sometimes longer—when the venture is finally ready to exit via IPO or a larger company's acquisition or merger.

5. *Don't shy away from revolutionary investments. Just be sure you understand them.*

This, too, is the very essence of venture capital investment. We aggressively seek revolutionary investments. We subscribe to PayPal and Palantir co-founder Peter Thiel's strategy of investing only in ideas and companies that appear to have home run potential.

Thiel's philosophy, which we share, is to consider, "What important truth do you see that very few people agree with you on?" We concur with him that if you see it first and others do not yet see it, you can start a company and build a monopoly position before others can get too close to your heels. That's what revolutionary investment is about. For Buffett, that has meant seemingly surprising affinity to solar and wind energy. For Len's teams, it has meant nanotechnology, disruptive advances in data storage, and uniquely new approaches to cancer treatment.

6. *Look for companies with top brands and the ability to "control" prices.*

This rule admittedly is a tougher one for us to claim comparability with Warren Buffett on. We don't invest in leading established brands like Buffett has done with American Express, the *Washington Post*, GE, Coca-Cola, and Wrigley. But our practices still do hold some similarity with Buffett's. We seek products and technologies with the sorts of preemptive marketplace insulation that will permit them to capture and hold leadership positions and set the kind of pricing that enables rich margins and lucrative profit potential.

7. *Always be liquid. Have a source of low-cost money ready to invest.*

Like Buffett, we strive to have cash available, or investors ready to entrust additional amounts to us quickly, to pounce on outstanding investment opportunities as quickly as the marketplace demands. Also like the Oracle of Omaha, we don't borrow to enable such liquidity.

Nevertheless, it is much more difficult for us than for Warren Buffett to achieve and ensure such advantageous liquidity and flexibility. Our investments do not pay dividends, and we do not own positions that generate cash flow for us like Buffett enjoys from his operating companies, especially his insurance companies. Moreover, venture capital funds intentionally stop raising new funds and making new investments at a point, as part of their charter is to liquidate their investments and return all those resulting monies to investors at the end of a predetermined period, hopefully returning a substantial multiple of the amount investors provided in the first place.

   8. *Be very selective. You don't have to move on every opportunity.*

We couldn't agree more with Mr. Buffett on this rule. We are inundated with potential deals, and generally act on perhaps one out of a hundred. A key to Len's funds' consistently outstanding performance over 30+ years has been discriminating deal selection. His teams don't do a lot of deals. We move only on those we believe have home run potential.

Our team's philosophy has always been, if we miss what turns out to be a great deal, *c'est la vie.* We are *not* motivated by FOMO—Fear of Missing Out. We are motivated far more by determination to minimize losing deals, though, of course, like any venture capital investor, we have our fair share. Fortunately, our fair share of losing deals (historically 63%) is much lower than industry averages of 80–85%.

   9. *Keep doing the above in good times and in bad.*

Again we are in lockstep with Mr. Buffett. We do not let macroeconomic cycles get in our way. Like Buffett, we are in it for the long run, not trying to time the market.

Of course, we do try to live by the mantra "buy low, sell high." However, the ventures that we pursue tend to be at such early stages that their valuations when we invest are not impacted much by broader market valuations. Further, since our investments typically percolate for 5–10 years before an exit, we don't pretend to have any idea of where the stock market and other measures will be in 5–10 years.

When our portfolio ventures are ready to exit, IPO prices can of course be impacted by near-term stock market froth or doldrums as well as by recent exits for comparable ventures. That might delay an exit opportunity for a little while in hopes of a more favorable market environment. Hopefully, even then the IPO price is such a substantial multiple of the initial investment that our investors are delighted.

Moreover, our strategic tendency to focus on Midwestern ventures, for which exits through acquisition by established businesses have some likelihood, also tends to insulate our portfolio ventures somewhat from short-term market gyrations even as they are ready to exit. This is because the price realized from acquisitions by established businesses tends to be driven more by the exiting venture's intrinsic long-term value than by the immediate state of the stock market.

10. *Minimize your mistakes, and learn from the ones you make.*

That's one more principle where we feel strong concurrence with the Oracle of Omaha. We discussed earlier the importance of discriminating deal selection—rigorous screening and due diligence. Better to miss some big winners than to lose our investors' money on too many losing deals. A key to minimizing mistakes in venture capital investment is to avoid FOMO mentality. It's also essential to learn from the mistakes you do make. Experience is vital in venture capital investment, just as it is in conventional equity investment or in most professional fields.

When you need surgery, you want to go to the seasoned pro who has done the same operation dozens, if not hundreds, of times. Actual data support that principle. In fact, the data show that use of a doctor who focuses on the particular type of surgery you need, versus going to a more general surgeon who's done many of your particular surgery but also many of lots of other types of surgery as well, indeed correlates with greater surgical success and fewer complications. This is why our sole focus is on venture capital. We don't dabble in other forms of private equity or real estate investment.

Unfortunately, venture capital investment experience is sometimes gained by losing a lot of money, which is not surprising in a field where on average 80–85% of deals wind up losing. It is estimated that it takes around $15 million in losses to train a successful professional VC investor. So, just as those delighted Berkshire Hathaway shareholders owe their good fortune to Warren Buffett's now-60+ years of experience, you can improve your venture capital investment success odds by relying on seasoned pros and staying away from less experienced VCs.

Why Venture Capital Returns Can Beat Even Warren Buffett

At this point, you may be asking the question, if the principles of successful venture capital investment are so similar to Buffett's rules, why should one expect the effective VC to be able to go beyond matching Buffett's performance and to beat his results? The answer is based on the very essence of venture capital investment.

One simple reason the effective VC should be reasonably expected to have a shot at beating Buffett long-term is that venture capital investment is inherently a high-risk/high-reward endeavor. The superior returns possible through venture capital, on average, appropriately offset the inherent risk.

Over 30+ years, Len's teams' investments have lost 63% of the time, which is lots better than the industry average of 80–85% but a much greater ratio of losses than for Warren Buffett. However, smart venture capital investment presents the opportunity for a percentage of deals to deliver returns of greater than 10× the initial investment and sometimes even 40× or 50× the initial investment. While Mr. Buffett's performance over 60+ years has been extraordinary, the kinds of returns we can achieve periodically in venture capital (i.e., 10× to all the way up to 40–50× initial investment within 5 to 10 years) realistically are impossible when you're investing in mature businesses like GEICO, American Express, railroads such as Union Pacific and Norfolk Southern, or everyday consumer products giants like Coca-Cola, Wrigley, and Kraft Heinz.

Buffett's investments in mature industries are tailored to deliver more consistent and predictable returns. He looks to buy consistently strong performers when their stock, or maybe the whole stock market, is temporarily out of favor, and then to hold those investment positions for the long-term, magnifying potential returns as well as their reliability. While he does invest in highly innovative and even revolutionary areas like solar and wind power, even such investments tend to be through mature vehicles like GE.

That is fundamentally different from venture capital's focus on startups and early stage businesses, before they reach the public trading markets and whose very reason for being is to capitalize on new technologies and often new markets. Remember the chart from the previous chapter that characterized risk and potential return by venture stage, from startup through expansion and later pre-IPO stages? Return potential can be viewed in a similar way in comparing the risks and potential rewards of investing in venture capital versus investing in mature publicly traded companies. (See Figure 5.1.)

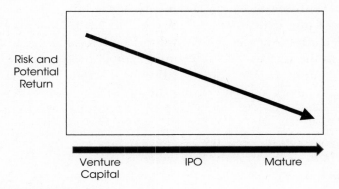

Figure 5.1   The Risk/Reward Tradeoff

This is why experienced, strategically optimized, prudently managed venture capital investment can beat even the returns generated so brilliantly over the past half-century by the Oracle of Omaha.

CHAPTER

6

Avoid the Seduction of Unicorns: Get in Early

The world has been captivated by the growing number of unicorns—private companies theoretically valued at more than $1 billion based on their latest round of funding. According to *CB Insights*, as of October 2016, there were 176 unicorns globally, with a cumulative valuation of $628 billion. Ninety-nine of them were in the United States, led by Uber, with a valuation of $66 billion. Number-two among U.S.-based unicorns is Airbnb, valued at $30 billion. If you were an early investor in any of these jewels, you're likely to win big! Get ready to pop the champagne. But what about investors who got in later, especially in the very latest fundraising rounds? How worthwhile are those investments going to be?

It's All High Risk, So Get in Early When the Biggest Returns Are Possible

We've said it before, but it's so fundamental that please pardon us for repeating it several times throughout this book—venture capital investing is a high-risk/high-potential-reward endeavor. Most deals wind up losing, often the entire amount invested. The industry norm is for about 15–20% of deals to generate some gain.

Our firms have exercised extreme selectivity and due diligence rigor, investing in only about 40 companies over the past 33 years. We've invested only in ventures we love. Our success rate shows the fruits of that concentration; it's double the industry norm, at 37%. Four of the ventures we supported have even become billion-dollar+ home runs. Nevertheless, that still means that, despite all-star performance, nearly two-thirds of our deals have lost money. Roughly 50% have been total losses.

The formula for venture capital investment success is to hit some big home runs, deals that return 10, 20, 30, or more times the amount invested. That requires selecting highly promising ventures *early*, while valuations are still low.

Notwithstanding the success of Len's multiple firms over the past 30+ years with an unconventionally small number of investments, our counsel for most individual investors would be to select a number of early-stage ventures for some diversification. While you can do that by investing in our pooled account that participates in all of our deals, we even understand when our investors invest as well with other firms, though in our heart of hearts we think they would be better served just to wait for more of our current firm's selections.

To be clear, we're not talking about individuals adopting a mutual fund–type (or worse yet, a passive index–type) approach to venture capital, investing in dozens of ventures. That's not the way to win at venture capital. We're talking about investing in perhaps five or six really high-potential ventures that you love. While there's no guarantee that they all won't lose, we do believe the odds should be with you and that this approach of extreme selectivity will pay handsome dividends long term.

Excessive Unicorn Valuations: All the Risk without the Big Reward Potential

Let's get back to the subject of unicorns. Many unicorns have already achieved notable marketplace success and will undoubtedly survive and even thrive over the long term. Nevertheless, even in the case of those making considerable strides in the marketplace, some of their current valuations strain credulity. We believe that, in many cases, their late-round investors risk vulnerability to substantial losses, just like with early-stage deals, but without the huge return multiples possible with early-stage deals. We may be proven wrong, but really, how likely is a big win when the venture is already valued at $10 billion or $20 billion or even $50 billion or more?

Let's look at Uber and its latest financing round valuation of $66 billion. According to *Bloomberg Technology*, Uber's net revenue for the first half of 2016 reached about $2 billion. By *net revenue*, we mean the revenue they keep after the drivers are paid. At the bottom line, for the first half of 2016, Uber lost $1.2 billion *before* interest, taxes, depreciation, and amortization. In 2015, Uber lost at least $2 billion before interest, taxes, depreciation, and amortization. Uber, which is seven years old, has lost at least $4 billion in the history of the company.

Admittedly a portion of those losses will go away now that Uber has closed down its business in China in exchange for a 17.5% stake in China-based ride-hailing leader Didi Chuxing as well as a $1 billion investment in Uber from Didi Chuxing. However, it has been reported that Uber also slid back into a loss position in its lead U.S. market in the second quarter of 2016.

While Uber still has many markets left to conquer and its achievements to date are indeed impressive, do those results really point to a future justifying a $66 billion valuation? Remember, a future value of anything less than $66 billion will mean a financial loss for Uber's latest investors.

How about Airbnb, America's second-highest-valued unicorn, with a valuation of $30 billion? According to *San Francisco Business Times*, Airbnb revenues were estimated at $900 million in 2015 and in late 2016 were projected at $1.7 billion for the year. Experts' best guess is that they are not yet profitable. Yes, they're still growing rapidly, but they're also already well known and broadly used. So are they really going to grow so much and so profitably as to be worth $30 billion? That's nearly as much as the market capitalization of the vast Marriott Hotels operation. It's possible, but do you really want to risk your money on that bet? And even if it does sustain such a value, how much opportunity is there for further gain?

What about Palantir, that secretive data-crunching resource to the FBI, CIA, and other mega-institutions? With 2015 revenues estimated by CNBC at $1.5 billion and its employees already housed in nearly two dozen Silicon Valley buildings, is it really going to continue to grow at such a pace and to such a scale as to be worth $20 billion?

You could go on and on, but the point is simple. Are these 99 U.S.-based unicorns really worth their nosebleed valuations? Or are their valuations being driven to excessive levels due to: (1) too much institutional money chasing after too few significant growth opportunities; (2) too many institutions and uber-wealthy folks wanting the bragging rights of claiming some ownership in these rock-star businesses; or (3) just plain old FOMO (Fear of Missing Out)?

Business Valuation 101

This isn't meant to be a dry textbook. If you're thinking about investing in venture capital, chances are you wrapped up your formal education long ago. So we've purposely stayed away thus far from academic-type lecturing. But a quick review of some traditional fundamentals regarding business valuation may help you think through this subject in order to reach your own point of view about unicorns and, more generally, about venture capital investment.

Finance experts traditionally define a business's value as the net present value of projected future discounted cash flows. For those of you without an academic grounding in the world of finance, let us try to explain what that means.

If you were thinking about buying a business and needed to figure out what was a fair price, you'd want to know how much money the business was expected to generate for you going forward. That would be your return on investment. You'd certainly want to get back more than you put in. Otherwise, why buy?

So you'd use your best understanding of the business situation and your plans for the business to project how much could be returned to you—the business's future cash flow. You'd also need to recognize what it would cost you to come up with the cash to buy the business. For example, if you borrowed money, how much would the interest on your loan cost? If you used cash you already held, what would you be giving up in terms of a return you could generate by investing that money in some other way?

You'd also need to consider the risk, because buying any business is never risk-free. That's why when businesses borrow money, for example, by selling bonds, the interest they pay is more than, say, what the U.S. government would pay on its bonds. The business's ability to survive and thrive and pay back the loan is a riskier bet than counting on the U.S. government to pay its obligations.

Considering these factors—the cost (real or opportunity-based) as well as the risk premium—you'd come up with what economists call a discount rate. For example, if you decided the appropriate discount rate was 10%, then an investment today of $1 would require a return a year later of $1.10 to make the risk of the investment worthwhile. If you had to wait two years for a return, you'd want to get back at least $1.21 ($1 + 10%/year compounded annually).

Even though you've been hearing about minuscule interest rates on things like U.S. Treasury bills, and even home mortgages have been available for years now with interest rates below 5%, large U.S. companies considering a substantial investment for a factory or to buy a smaller company might consider an appropriate discount rate (i.e., their cost of capital plus a risk premium) of perhaps 10–20%, depending on the relative risk of the investment under consideration.

Applying Business Valuation 101 to Venture Capital Investment

Let's look at an illustration applying this textbook approach to your consideration of venture capital investment. Let's say that you invest $25,000. You recognize that this investment is not liquid and that you are likely to wait five to seven years for a return. We'll assume that you're going to get your payout in seven years. We'll further assume that you require an expected return of 15%/year to justify the risk of investing in venture capital. To achieve a return of 15%/year on your initial investment (i.e., your $25,000 must grow by 15%/year, compounded annually) you'll need to get back $66,500. That's 2.66 times your original investment. If you want to see for yourself, pull out a calculator and run through the numbers.

Let's say that your $25,000 investment is deployed by the VC firm in equal amounts of $5,000 in five separate ventures, and that four of those ventures are total losses. That means that the one winning $5,000 investment would need to return all $66,500, a multiple of 13.3 times that single investment. That's reasonably typical of what would be considered a highly successful outcome among individual venture deals. That's how money is made in venture capital. You expect most the venture deals to lose, but expect and hope that at least one will strike some gold.

Many VCs will tell you that this kind of traditional valuation methodology is impractical for venture capital. There's just too much uncertainty and too much that seems immeasurable. They suggest that venture capital valuations rely on perceived potential along with passionate commitment and a dose of hope.

They may be right about that for the individual investor investing in a single deal, that crunching all the numbers in textbook fashion is an impractical exercise. Nevertheless, at the end of the day, when you make an investment, you do need to consider the return you expect, or hope, to receive at some time in the future, as well as the risk you are taking. And you hope the VC investing your money in multiple deals is thinking along those lines.

In venture capital investment, you recognize the riches of potential success, but need to discount those hoped-for future values sharply to reflect inherent risk. Of course, if you invest in a number of deals, or in a pooled fund that in turn invests in a number of deals, that diversification manages and reduces your overall risk.

Try Applying That Logic to Unicorns

Let's say you decide that, instead of investing in a pooled fund focused on early-stage investments, you will invest in a fund focused on unicorns. We'll further assume your $25,000 is divided equally among five unicorns. Since these unicorns are much further along in their development, you expect to get your payout in just two years. We'll assume you're hoping for the same 15%-per-year gain. That would require a payout after two years of $33,063. Try the math: $25,000 plus 15% after a year, and then plus another 15% after the second year.

Let's further assume that two of those five unicorns drop in value by 25%, one returns the $5,000 initially invested, and two of the five account for all of your gain. Those two would need to double in value over the two years to meet your overall 15%/year return objective. Do you want to place such a bet? We wouldn't.

Before you accuse us of stacking the deck just to support our position, you need to recognize that those assumptions about drops in unicorn values aren't crazy. According to *Fortune.com*, during 2016 Morgan Stanley marked down on its books, relative to latest fundraising-round valuations, the value of its holdings of three of the largest unicorns—Palantir by 32%, Flipkart (India-based) by 27%, and Dropbox by 25%. Others similarly marked down on their books the values of much-publicized VC-funded ventures. Fidelity slashed the values on its books on its holdings of Dropbox, Snapchat, and Zenefits. T. Rowe Price marked down the value of its Dropbox holdings by more than 50%. Unicorn valuations don't always go up. Some also go down.

Why Many Unicorn Valuations Don't Make Sense to Us

The problem with some unicorns' soaring valuations is that they seem to assume the stars are perfectly aligned and everything will go right. That rarely happens. Yes, it may have for Microsoft, Google, and Facebook, three huge winners over the past 40 years. But how many of those are there? Even Apple had to survive near disaster before its remarkable success.

In order for it to make sense to us, Uber's $66 billion valuation would require that its annual earnings before interest, taxes, depreciation, and amortization ultimately reach and sustain at somewhere around $3 to $5 billion per year. That's in the range where their revenues are today, and they're hardly at an infant stage, already enjoying broad followings in many markets. We recognize that self-driving cars may eventually drive up Uber profit margins. However, what if governmental regulations block portions of the company's planned expansion? What if, before self-driving cars are available broadly, Uber drivers are ruled to be employees rather than independent contractors, changing the company's fundamental economics? What if municipalities figure out ways to level the playing field for conventional taxis versus Uber cars? The risks are real. We wouldn't bet on a $66 billion value, never mind hoping for a big gain to justify the investment risk in the first place.

How about Airbnb's $30 billion valuation? Again, they're hardly an infant startup; 2016 revenue is estimated at less than $2 billion, and they are not believed to yet be profitable. Again, fundamental risks to their economic model are substantial. For example, on October 21, 2016, New York Governor Andrew Cuomo signed state legislation that would impose a fine of up to $7,500 on anyone advertising a short-term (less than 30 days) rental apartment on a home-sharing website. If either of us lived in New York, that sure would discourage us from listing our apartment on Airbnb, even though we'd love the rental income if perhaps one of us were going to be away for some period of time.

While many homeowners, renters, and travelers love Airbnb and use it repeatedly, others have had the kinds of disappointing experiences you wouldn't have in a name-brand hotel and so won't be back. More importantly, many cities are wrestling with Airbnb properties' lack of compliance with their lodging-related laws and regulations, especially their lodging/hotel tax requirements, which in many cases are not being followed. Similarly, many condominium associations and co-op boards are wrestling with enforcing more tightly their rules and regulations restricting or prohibiting currently active Airbnb rentals.

These sorts of risks really call into question for us the wisdom of Airbnb's $30 billion valuation, never mind hoping for a big, relatively short-term gain on an investment at anywhere near the current valuation.

Unicorns Having Difficulty Exiting and Delivering Investor Returns

You may hear a lot about how these unicorns are staying private because they want to. Some will profess that they just don't want the short-term market pressures of public ownership.

That's undoubtedly true for some, but we think there may be a different problem as well for some others behind their remaining private for longer than expected. The marketplace simply may not be interested in some of these unicorns at the prices their owners expect and are hoping for. Given the billions of dollars invested in unicorns, many of their investors are probably eager for exits in order to realize a return on their investments. Their reluctance to accept haircuts on those investments, selling for less than they had paid, may be what is getting in the way.

The mergers-and-acquisitions (M&A) scene for unicorns has been particularly bleak. That's not because of a lack of potential acquirer appetite for large, high-potential tech companies. According to *CB Insights*, as of late 2016 there had been 21 acquisitions of private tech companies during the year for over $1 billion. Unfortunately for the unicorn owners, only 2 had been unicorns, valued in their last fundraising round at $1 billion+. We're guessing that a number of the unicorns may have wanted to be acquired, but that their share price expectations were too high to tempt suitors.

The respected venture capital industry tracking resource *CB Insights* believes, as we do, that many unicorn valuations, and hence price expectations, are simply too high. Those valuations were based on growth expectations that now in many cases seem far too optimistic. As *CB Insights* put it, they are "priced for perfection," and, as we suggested earlier, such perfection—such ideal alignment of all the relevant forces—rarely happens.

Unicorn valuations have been inflated so high that, in the world of corporate buyers, who tend to act much more based on the "Business Valuation 101" approach described earlier, there is little M&A appetite until valuations drop back down to levels that prospective buyers can make sense of. *CB Insights* points out that, "in some cases, private market unicorns are actually valued at much higher multiples than their public market counterparts." Ironically perhaps, due to these exit hurdles, there is pressure on some unicorns to accelerate achievement of positive cash flow, a pragmatic shift that will reduce growth rates and could preclude achievement of the lofty growth expectations that drove the valuations in the first place.

Now You Know Why We Believe in Early-Stage Investment

Now you've seen why we're not interested in investing in ventures already valued at $1 billion+, where a return multiple of 2 or 3 looks unlikely and a return of 10 or 20 times investment seems virtually impossible. Gambling in Las Vegas would probably be a better bet.

We believe in the more traditional venture capital success formula, focusing on early fundraising rounds—often after venture potential is qualified through angel/seed funding but before valuations escalate wildly. For early-stage investments, where ventures may be valued at $5 or $10 million, or even $10 to $20 million, while most fail, success could mean an exit valuation in the tens or even hundreds of millions of dollars. Four of the ventures we've supported over 33 years have even exited at $1 billion or more, though, of course, you can't count on that.

This early-stage focus has worked well for our investors over three decades. While the VC industry's average deal success rate (i.e., achieving any positive return on investment) is in the 15–20% range, through rigorous screening and due diligence, our success rate has been 37%. Our gross IRR in aggregate has been 28%. To get there requires some exits at 10, 20, or more times the initial investment to offset the nearly two-thirds of our deals that lose.

Our Concerns for the Venture Capital Industry and Individual Investors

Getting in on a unicorn round is great for bragging rights, but for late-stage investors, getting out with a profit can be tough. We're betting that FOMO results in lots of loudly bursting unicorn bubbles.

Nevertheless, we're not concerned about a repeat of 2000's broad dot-com bubble, which hit dozens of high-flying, young, publicly traded companies, devastating the finances of millions of Americans. Today's soaring valuations belong to companies that are still private. Their investors are primarily institutions and ultra-wealthy individuals who can weather the risk, so impact should be contained.

We are concerned, though, that a series of loud unicorn bubble bursts could cool the flow of investment dollars feeding life-changing innovation. That would be unfortunate, since conditions for tech-enabled startups have never been better. It would be especially unfortunate for the estimated ten million accredited investors (defined by the SEC as having net worth of $1 million+ excluding primary residence or ongoing annual income over $200,000), who finally—thanks to the JOBS Act—have access to professionally managed venture capital investment.

We believe that following the traditional early-stage venture capital investment approach will continue to generate attractive returns for investors who partner with proven professional management and practice appropriate deal diversification. In contrast, we're betting that late-stage investors in unicorn deals will increasingly find themselves under water.

CHAPTER 7

Finding the Highest Quality Investments at the Right Price

Venture capital investing is a difficult business. An investor must be smart, lucky, and know how to play the game to achieve outsized returns.

We told you earlier that venture capital fund returns have averaged about 12% per year over the long term and 19.7% over the past 20 years according to the Thomson Reuters Venture Capital Research Index. Nevertheless, returns on individual deals, and even on pooled funds holding a number of ventures, can vary considerably from negative to highly positive.

Len's various funds and investment pools over 30+ years have delivered gross annual returns ranging from 14% to 159%. We had to be both good and lucky to never have a losing fund.

Investing in individual deals, though, is difficult, and that's what VC firms do. The venture capital industry norm is that only about 15–20% of all investments will make any money at all, and about half of those money makers will be considered home runs, returning five times the money invested or greater. As we've said more than once in this book (sorry for the repetition, but we're proud of our record), our record is better, with over a third of our investments making some money and almost half of those money makers considered big home runs, with either an IRR of 100%+ or a return multiple on the money invested of greater than 10. Four of our investments and/or companies that we have helped start have reached values of over $1 billion, with America Online at one time having a market capitalization of over $350 billion!

Our average annual gross IRR over 30+ years is 28%, beating Warren Buffett's 20%+ IRR (although he has done this for 50 years). To accomplish such high returns, we had to find the highest quality investments at the right price, and then exit the investments smartly for an excellent gain. Some would say that this is just another form of "buying low and selling high." However, in venture capital investing, this often-sage financial advice grossly oversimplifies the challenges and can easily miss the highest quality investment opportunities.

The AOL Story

Earlier in this book, we told you just a bit about the difficulties encountered by the founder of a company in the early 1980s called Control Video Corporation. In discussing the importance of timing, we explained that this unfortunate founder seemed to be a little ahead of his time with his venture. His venture was launched with the idea of downloading video games over regular (i.e., traditional landline) phone lines through a low-cost modem plugged into an Atari video game console, which would then display the games for play on the consumer's television.

We'd now like to tell you more of this story, as it will illustrate some of the challenges of finding, and in this case also intervening aggressively to enable, the highest quality investments. The initial company, Control Video Corporation (CVC), was funded with about $12 million in venture capital (one of the most aggressively funded VC-backed startups to that time), supported by a number of the then-major U.S. venture capital firms, including Kleiner Perkins, Allstate (where Len began his venture capital career), Citibank, Inco, Merrill Piccard, Union Bank, and others.

A major marketing and media blitz was launched, and the product/service was sold at Sears (Sears was America's largest retailer at the time) and other major retail outlets (as there was no functional Internet at the time). The visionary idea was not only to offer the then-very-popular video games on demand essentially in real time, but to piggyback on the booming sales of the Atari 3600 Video Game Console and popular games such as Frogger, Space Invaders, and Pitfall.

Unfortunately, the only real pitfall was Control Video itself, which, after burning through all of its investors' capital and owing suppliers another $18 million, essentially crashed and burned, representing a major setback for the venture capital industry itself, which was just beginning to recover from a long dry spell. To the seemingly astute VC investment groups, Control Video initially seemed like a high-quality investment opportunity at a reasonable entry price, but it went badly wrong and could have stopped the building momentum of the entire VC industry.

When all seemed lost, Allstate, Citibank, and Inco's venture capital groups stepped up and, in support of and along with the company, including its management team, invested even more to buy the company more time, and renamed the company Quantum Computer, which was later renamed again, to America Online (AOL). Prior to AOL's historic 2001 merger with Time Warner, the now-struggling company (recently acquired by Verizon for $4.4 billion) was valued at a lofty $163 billion, and after the merger was valued at an even loftier $350 billion+, representing the most amazing turnaround in venture capital history and the largest business merger ever. AOL shareholders did very well indeed, with several making billions and about 10,000 making $1 million or better, and this ignited a tech boom in the Washington D. C. area that continues to this day.

You may ask, was Control Video Corporation a high-quality investment at the right price? It would have been tough to call it a high-quality investment at the right price after the venture capital leaders initially invested $12 million and saw the venture essentially crash and burn. However, this case study illustrates vividly the value that venture capitalists can bring to the fore, ultimately enabling phenomenal returns even if it looked like a bad bet for a while.

That initial investment brought together a team of dedicated VC investors, who then brought in an experienced turnaround expert, restructured the company, and recruited a new management team that redefined and redirected the business. That redefinition repurposed the modem technology originally intended to bring video games into the home, instead ushering in the era of in-home Internet connectivity, via telephone dialup. While we'd laugh today at the painfully slow data transmission rate, AOL was the pioneer leading us to today's overloaded email inbox. Our point here is that the venture capitalists themselves were instrumental in the investment going from a total loss to a return in the billions.

So, were the VCs right or wrong about their initial investment in Control Video? Notwithstanding misguided early steps, the key VC investors had the vision to see that the personal computer was coming to desktops broadly, that low-cost communications modems would get faster and cheaper, and that the convergence of personal computers and ultimately higher speed modems would result in an online information and communications explosion. They got the central business idea right, but it took several tries, a different management team, and more capital investment to execute the idea. It also required patience, taking a number of years of effort as the pc/modem combo took time to be on everyone's desktop.

Timing, as in many VC investments, proved to be critical. If an investor invests too early in the market development cycle, a loss is likely; too late and a loss is for sure. Entry timing must often be just right for a high-quality VC investment to emerge.

In the case of CVC/Quantum/AOL, the initial price proved not to really matter, as AOL became a historic home run. Price paid on investment tends to matter if the exit results in a single or double, or maybe even a home run that just barely clears the fence, but it matters a lot less in a grand-slam exit. Investors in CVC/Quantum/AOL did, however, need great persistence and deep pockets to continue investing over a decade until success was achieved. Those that held the stock even after the company went public in 1994, at about a $70 million market capitalization, also needed the fortitude to hold the stock until 2001, the year of the merger with Time Warner, when the market capitalization hit a high exceeding $350 billion. In this case, patience, persistence, and creativity were the keys to the highest quality investment at what must ultimately be judged to have been the right price.

How to Manage Risk, Play the Odds, and Win in an Evolving Market

Now and again, as Jim Kimsey, former AOL chairman and CEO, used to say, "Finding a pony in a pile" is mostly lucky, and "making a pony from a pile" is even rarer. So, is there a key to successfully finding the highest quality VC investments at the right price—a proven method of seeking, finding, and closing these rare investment gems? How do the most successful VC investors find their way to the best deals and highest returns?

The first fundamental is to understand the essence of venture capital investing and how different it is from other classes of investments. Unlike Warren Buffett's investments, which leverage predictability, recognizing a company's greater intrinsic value relative to its price, whether through quick asset liquidation or sustained long-term cash generation, a key element in venture capital investing is the inherent risk in each investment.

Because of that inherent risk, for many years the road to the highest returns was thought to be diversification of VC investments in a fund or investment pool. A venture capital firm, generally using institutional monies, would pool these funds and over four to seven years make 15 to perhaps 30 initial investments in the pool, and then make follow-on investments in those ventures that were performing up to expectations and continued to show attractive potential. With this approach, generally about 85% of the investments made no money at all, another 10% or so perhaps doubled or tripled their money, and the remaining 5% or so—one to three investments—were true home runs, returning over ten times the money invested.

This diversified approach returned about 12% annually on average for all VC investing over about a 50-year period. This proved to be a reasonably predictable investment approach, particularly if investments were made over a number of funds over different economic cycles. One fund might have a negative return, another in the middle, and another a home run fund. There was high volatility among the pieces, but reasonably predictable returns in the aggregate for the risk.

Recently, this extreme diversification approach has come under fire from a number of highly successful venture capital investors, including the famed PayPal founder and Facebook investor, Peter Thiel. Thiel argues in his insightful book, *Zero to One* (published in 2014 by The Crown Publishing Group), that, rather than following such a diversification method, which accepts that 80–85% of all the deals will fail, one would do better by making fewer investments in the first place, and then going on to focus intensively all effort and capital on the few that appear increasingly likely to become the home runs. He advocates far greater selectivity right from the start, only investing in the first place in ideas and companies that appear to have true home run potential.

For this home run method to work, the investor must have access to and the ability to spot or create likely home run investments, and not just one but rather seven or eight to have the house odds of at least one true home run materializing. We subscribe to this same philosophy. That's why we review literally a hundred or more opportunities for every deal we ultimately select for investment.

Prior to 2000, there were a number of investment banks that would undertake an initial public offering (IPO) for a fledgling company that, while having revenue, still had no earnings. In fact, at the height of the Internet bubble, even revenue was often not needed. Some of these companies could result in a single, a double, or perhaps even a triple for the IPO investor. Again, a broad portfolio diversification could work to achieve a 12% annual average IRR.

Unfortunately, though, many IPO investors were not so diversified and lost heavily. After the dot-com bubble burst in 2000, many of these investment banks went out of business, so these smaller IPOs were no longer possible. Without them, the likelihood that the traditional venture portfolio diversification strategy would work, or was even readily feasible, disappeared.

During this same period, as more and more capital went into venture capital investing to feed the Internet frenzy, driving valuations and share prices ever higher, it became necessary for VC firms to invest larger and larger amounts of capital in each investment. In this superheated investment climate, the only ventures that could produce major returns and permit a VC firm to stay competitive were the home runs.

What It Takes to Hit Investment Home Runs

How then can an investor new to venture capital succeed? If it really takes home runs, what features signal that an investment has such potential? The most probable route to investment success would seem to be to invest with a major venture capital firm that has had considerable success year in and year out for several decades. This is the way that institutional investors try to invest in venture capital.

For individual investors, however, other than the mega-wealthy, this approach until now has been almost impossible, as the 25 or so most notably successful VC firms rarely admit individual investors. When they do, often in "sidecar" funds with their institutional investors, these funds are limited to the lucky, the best connected, and the few.

Accessibility to individuals is finally here, though, through the establishment over the past few years of several online venture capital firms, including Angel List, Our Crowd, Funder's Club, Circle Up, and VCapital, founded by one of the authors (Len), with the other (Ken) serving in an advisory capacity. These online firms generally offer both individual investment deals and pooled investment funds.

Some of the firms perform extensive due diligence for greater selectivity in the investments they offer while others appear to perform somewhat less. Some of the firms have extensive experience in VC investing and some considerably less. Since online VC investing is so new, these online firms have little return history or realized IRR performance data based on actual exits to provide an investor with confidence. So the individual investor needs to understand the features and makeup of a likely home run investment, and how to track them down, or more realistically recognize the venture capital firms that have the ability to find those home run opportunities.

Hitting a home run requires the VC investor to see opportunity and potential before others do. If she's too late and that potential has already become evident to lots of others, the share price will have already escalated, making home run returns that much tougher.

In his quest to recognize opportunity (at the right price) before others do, Thiel likes the idea of considering, "What important truth do you see that very few people agree with you on?" To find those investment gems, Thiel's approach is to focus on a very large market or technical opportunity that few others see or understand well. If you see it first and others do not yet see it, or understand it better than others, you can start a company and build a strong, sustainable leadership position before anyone else is out of the gate.

The ventures that recognize those important truths also need "compelling economics." The business idea or product needs to be at least 50% cheaper than the competition, or 50% faster, or 50% more compelling overall; a 100% advantage is even better. A good example is the authors' recent home run investment in Chicago-based Cleversafe. Cleversafe's technological innovations in big data storage and security disrupted the data storage market by cutting data storage costs up to 80%, combined with significantly enhanced security, leading to IBM's recent acquisition of the company for $1.3 billion. Find a rare idea or product whose potential others do not yet see and will not see anytime soon, that has compelling economics, and the investors could be well on the way to a home run.

Visualizing this rare idea or product, in the words of the poet Tennyson, takes "seeing as far as the eye can see and knowing all the wonder that will be." For a successful VC investor, a sense of wonder at all the possibilities is essential. But so also is a profound skepticism that all dreams come true, as most don't.

A VC investor must also discipline himself to visualize only about 10 to perhaps 15 years out, as this is about the patience limit of society and the financial community for high-risk investments. A longer time horizon will permit competition not even dreamed of to emerge. Most technologies that will prove successful over the next 30 years have not yet even been imagined.

While 10 to 15 years may seem awfully long, the window for successful VC visualization itself can be short, as others' visualization can spawn competition that must be beaten to the prize. Entrepreneurs and the VCs who back them are under an imperative to act immediately. Acting immediately for the VC means recognizing quickly those entrepreneurs whose vision and execution of that vision will be successful. This, too, requires vision. Success tends to come to those who follow the old adage, "It takes one to know one."

How to Find the Potential Home Runs

It may seem strange that, as venture capitalists, we see parallels in the path to success with the world's most notable traditional investor, Warren Buffett. Buffett's biggest investments have been in such traditional businesses as insurance companies, railroads, banks, newspapers, and the Coca-Cola Company. So, where's the parallel with the venture capital focus usually on high tech, which Buffett historically avoided because he didn't understand it?

As we reviewed a few chapters back, Warren Buffett has been a successful investor for 50+ years for a number of reasons, foremost that he only invests in what he knows, understands, and is comfortable with. He committed to that approach as a young boy, when he took the money he made from a paper route and invested it in a farm. Buffett has looked at and made so many good investments over many years (and, he'll admit, some poor ones too, just not too many of them) that his odds of visualizing a good investment are much higher than average. He has also had to learn where and in whom to place his trust. This intuitive investment sense allows him to know which investment opportunities to trust when he sees them, and whom to trust as well.

Just like for Warren Buffett, the successful VC invests in what he knows, understands, and is comfortable with. For us, that includes high tech in industry sectors such as information technology and biotechnology, where our team has extensive knowledge and background. A big part of this is also knowing and trusting the source of the opportunity. Most high-quality VC investment opportunities come to the VC through trusted sources—an attorney, accountant, broker-banker, tax advisor, consultant, or entrepreneur who has a prior relationship with the VC. The referral source often knows what will interest a particular VC as to industry focus, stage, and investment dollar requirements, as well as knowing if a particular entrepreneur is "backable."

Very few investments that are actually made come in blind over the transom. The old adage from Chicago politics not to hire anyone "that ain't sent" applies to VC investing as well. To find opportunities that could become successful investments, we listen carefully to trusted sources that have experience reviewing venture capital investments and often investing in them as well. Referral networks assist greatly in knowing whom to trust.

Knowing *what* to trust can be a bit trickier and brings into play both right- and left-brain cognitive skills. The left brain has traditionally been viewed as the seat of logical processing. Logical data processing for venture capital investing requires a robust and reasonably accurate data set as well as effective linear processing skills. Processing speed, beyond a point, is not very relevant, as accuracy and resulting insight should be valued over speed. Often it's better to wait than to hurry, as new data comes to the fore and sheds new light on the investment.

Right-brain processing is all about intuition. It is important to understand, though, that true intuition is based on experience. What one might call intuition, but which is separate from experience, is usually just wishing and hoping. That's not a smart basis for important investment decisions.

In VC investing, the logical processing work is mostly about deciding what data are most relevant to the decision to be made. Is the market size most important, or is what matters more the market growth rate, the superiority of the technology, the drive and persistence of the entrepreneur, the degree of difficulty in securing funds, the amount of funds required, speed to market, ability to scale quickly, potential for strong and sustainable leadership position, first-mover advantage, or some particular combination of those variables? Once the most relevant and critical questions are determined, then it's "Just the facts, please!"

Accurate intuition is a function of both temperament and experience. For an early-stage VC investor, including seed and startup investing, the most useful temperament tends toward a high comfort level with risk coupled with a hardheaded appreciation of the reality of likely failure. In early-stage investing there are rarely any hard numbers or even clear, indisputable facts.

Experience is especially vital. Unfortunately, experience is often gained by losing a big pile of money. It is estimated that it takes at least $15 million in losses to train a successful professional VC investor.

The individual investor doesn't need to go through such a process of accumulating experience through costly losses, though some choose to. We believe that for most individual investors, it makes more sense to hitch your wagon to a professional venture capital firm with an experienced team with a meaningful track record.

We recognize, though, that some individual investors prefer more of a do-it-yourself approach. For them, the same concept may make sense as for the young, aspiring, professional VC. If that's your preference, our advice would be to start out with small investments and work your way up to larger ones as your experience grows. There are online sites for accredited investors where the investment requirement can be as little as $1,000. Under the new provisions of Title III of the JOBS Act, even non-accredited individual investors can invest in venture capital on a limited basis, with these specific limitations:

- If either their annual income or net worth is less than $100,000, then the greater of $2,000 or 5% of the lesser of their annual income or net worth.
- If both their annual income and net worth are equal to or more than $100,000, investors are allowed to invest up to 10% of the lesser of their annual income or net worth.

Venture capital investing is both an art and a science. Science informs the art and art the science. But don't play aggressively until experience brings the skill to integrate art and science. The art is knowing whom to trust, when to trust, and what to trust.

Price Can Matter, Too, and Can Be Tricky

We've talked about the challenge of finding high-quality investments. Of secondary importance, but still potentially important (since most investments don't turn out like AOL), is the price paid for the investment. In the earlier decades of venture capital investing, it was considered unusual to put a value on a company with revenue of more than twice that revenue. For those companies that had little-to-no revenue, a value of between $4 and $10 million was considered generous by VC investors. A $1 million investment might then buy 10–25% of the company's fully diluted stock.

During the rise of the dot-com bubble, from 1995 to 2000, the price of early-stage ventures became more expensive. For example, in one case investors paid at a $15 million valuation for a company that had about $5 million in forward projected revenue, although admittedly inclusion of investors and customers the likes of Microsoft, Visa International, William Blair, and Paul Allen's VC firm added to the perceived value. The company, Software.net, initially based in Palo Alto with three employees over a barbershop, was eventually split into two companies, CyberSource and Beyond.com. Both undertook successful IPOs, with the initial early-stage investors in the combined entity receiving 41× their money invested in about three and a half years from the date of initial investment. So at the time of the initial investment, the $15 million valuation seemed high, but the reward of stepping up to the price was great. These were heady days for entrepreneurs and the valuations of their companies.

Beware, though, as valuations are constantly in flux in a VC market seeking the highest quality investments at low-to-fair prices. Valuations declined as the dot-com bubble burst, with many companies unable to find financing at any price, and those that could having to give up more of the company for less.

Even during that difficult era, though, those companies that were in a particularly hot industry or addressed a large and popular market could still maintain higher values. VCs will often pay a higher price if the so-called *comparables* are higher. Comparables are the exit values, either through an IPO or company sale or merger, of companies similar to the company being financed. The VC reasoning is that if a similar company will fetch an excellent price, then the company they are investing in should as well. No two companies are ever exactly similar, however, so with this valuation approach the investor should continue to beware.

A number of entrepreneurs have come to believe that the more traditional venture capital market will not treat them fairly as to valuation and will always seek to invest at the lowest possible price. These entrepreneurs then seek out other sources of financing, including angels, angel groups, and online funding.

While tough pricing and terms are often a feature of venture capital financing, venture capitalists will often pay up for a highly competitive deal that others are actively seeking. Pricing is essentially set by the supply and demand in the marketplace for VC funding, so it's essential for entrepreneurs to test the market for their stock through discussions with a number of potential investors and sources.

Today some VC firms view it as a competitive advantage in attracting the best and brightest entrepreneurs to be considered "nice" and willing to pay fair value. Frankly, fair pricing—not inflated or excessively low—makes sense for both sides of the transaction. If the share price is too high, then early-stage investors may insist on protection against ownership dilution in later funding rounds, which would likely come at the expense of the management team's ownership share. On the other hand, if the share price is too low, the entrepreneur and his team could lose motivation.

Need to Consider Non-monetary Costs, Too

There are both monetary costs and less readily quantified non-monetary costs in venture capital investing. For a venture capitalist, like for most businesspeople, time is money. If an investment is expected to take less time to exit and/or less of the venture capitalist's time in working on and adding value to an investment, the VC may be willing to pay a higher price. Also, if the investment is further along the development curve, either already having revenue or about to achieve revenue, the price paid will likely be higher, as the perceived risk of loss is lower.

If the perceived risk of loss is considered high, on the other hand, then the VC will generally require a lower price. That lower price is needed to offset the human cost of the time that will likely be required from the VC, as well as the economic cost to the VC to compensate for the greater likelihood of a loss, which can also be quite high as to reputation both inside and outside the VC firm.

Considering the human cost component, the VC needs to consider his potential required time commitment relative to using that time either to raise additional funds for the firm or to make new investments, so it is a real opportunity cost that must be considered.

Some Pricing Advice for the Entrepreneur

Experienced venture capital investors have a good idea of which industries are in fashion, and of the risk/reward profile for the particular industry and stage of the deal. They will also have a good idea of what price the deal may bring from another VC. Generally, it's best to find an investor who will pay a fair price (not necessarily the highest) and who brings other added value to the investment, including a workable, if not close, relationship with the entrepreneur.

The following approach has worked well for many aspiring fundraisers:

- Bring your deal along to the highest stage possible on your own prior to seeking venture capital. This will help maximize your price.
- Discuss possible valuations of your deal with your attorney, accountant, investment banker, and any friendly venture capitalists prior to establishing the price.
- Select a valuation that is reasonable in light of market realities, a bit on the higher side perhaps, so there is room to negotiate. Not so high, though, that the venture capitalist will feel that working with you is a waste of time.
- Try the valuation on several VCs, including at least one who would be a good prospect as a lead investor.
- If the valuation fails to pass "the snicker test" with several venture capitalists, revise the valuation downward.
- Remember that most VC-funded ventures require more than one round of equity infusion prior to positive cash flow or exit. Don't sell so much of the company that there is none left for the team.

If you sell one-third of your company for $1 million, the valuation or value of your company, at least on paper, is set at $3 million. Remember, the higher the perceived quality, the more likely the higher the price.

PART

III

For the Entrepreneur: A Guide to the Money Search and All That Follows

CHAPTER

8

The Mating Dance: Prospecting for a Venture Capital Investor

Since you're investing the time to read this, we assume you are either already a passionate entrepreneur or aspire to be one. You are also probably either an exceptional planner, not yet needing financing help but anticipating and preparing for that day, or you are already searching pretty urgently for additional funds. Even if you fall into that group of exceptional planners, if you do proceed in your entrepreneurial quest, you will be needing funds pretty urgently at some point, so let's proceed here on that basis.

We'll assume you are close to exhausting your personal funds and easily accessible credit and are near the end of the road in raising funds from family and friends. If you've reached out to bankers, you've learned that they're simply not interested unless you can demonstrate cash flow certainty, have substantial collateral, or can guarantee loans personally, which seems unlikely given our other assumptions.

You've heard about venture capitalists and figure that's your solution. Surely they'll see the brilliance of your idea and write the big check you need.

Unfortunately, you need to understand the realities:

- Most new ventures fail. (We know, you've heard that already countless times.) They are inherently risky. *You* are risky. (Sorry.)

- A major reason why most new ventures fail is that they are unable to raise the capital needed to buy time in order to fix problems and get all the pieces right.
- Discerning professional venture capitalists see roughly 100 proposals for every one they accept and invest in.

Yikes! It sounds impossible. Sorry for the cold, wet blanket.

Now for some good news. Securing the funds you seek will be hard, but it's not impossible. Those few who really understand the importance of risk capital, where to find it, and how to get it significantly enhance their chances of being among the survivors, building a successful company, and creating wealth.

Actually, Lots of Sources and Lots of Available Dollars

According to a *MoneyTree* Report from PricewaterhouseCoopers and the National Venture Capital Association, venture capital investments in aspiring ventures have totaled $50–$60 billion per year over the past couple of years. Somebody is securing funds!

According to FindTheCompany.com, there are around 1,200 venture capital firms to choose from. As we mentioned before, that includes some overseas firms as well as some that might be better characterized as angel groups, but there are 500–600 bona fide venture capital firms in America. Also, the angel groups might be appropriate for you at this point as well. Net, there are a lot of potential sources of the funds you need.

How to Appeal to the Venture Capitalist

You know how inherently risky new ventures are. Of course, we're sure that yours is different—after all, you will be making it happen. But you still need to keep in mind that, unfortunately, just based on the marketplace numbers, the odds are against you.

It is unlikely the venture capitalist will risk his investors' money on your venture unless you, your idea, and your potential company have substantial venture capital appeal. Here's what you'll need for that appeal:

- Have a good and hopefully sufficiently unique idea with the potential to make a lot of money.

- Be willing to give up a good portion of the return on your idea and efforts to compensate the venture capitalist and his investors for the risk they will take.
- Want to build a BIG successful company—at least $50–$100 million in revenue with a substantial profit margin.
- Be able to accomplish those results within five to ten years.
- Be willing to accept and work with the venture capitalist as a partner. (Remember, you couldn't pursue your dream without her money.)
- Know your high growth potential business domain very well, have already attracted the start of a talented supporting cast, and be capable of attracting other talented players as the needs of the business grow.
- Be willing to provide your venture investor with a viable exit for his investment within five to ten years.

This book will help you get your act together, take it on the road, and return home with the capital you need. While it will discuss at length how to sell yourself and your company, venture capitalists are experienced and skilled at finding real value in a situation. You won't be able to obtain capital just by being a skilled promoter and salesperson. You must present evidence of real value.

Prospecting for Gold, or, Better Yet, Drilling for Oil

Prospecting for venture capital gold can be as challenging as was prospecting for actual gold back in the gold rush. Many other miners are also searching for the mother lode. You will need a competitive advantage—all the known art plus some entrepreneurial inventiveness—to prevail.

Part of the known art is recognizing that there are far more effective and efficient approaches than the old miner's panning technique. That technique called for the miner to continuously slosh water around in the pan until the gold settled to the bottom. The equivalent today would be reaching out to all those 1,200 venture capital firms and angel groups, hat in hand, hoping for enough gold to settle in your venture. Raising the funds you need that way could take years—maybe your whole life—and you might still come up empty. And implementing your idea can't wait for years. The fast-moving marketplace waits for no one.

In order to have a reasonable shot at your venture reaching the market while there's still a market available to it, you'd be better off figuring out where the small number of highest potential sites are and digging intensively there, more like the way oil companies search for the few best places to drill for oil. This approach involves pursuing just five or six VCs, selected using the following three-step method:

1. Find the VCs located geographically near your company. Some venture capitalists may even want to walk or bike to your office or at least be able to drive there.
2. Narrow your list further by considering only those who invest actively in the deal stage where you're at. We'll review in a minute how the industry defines deal stages so you'll know the stage where you're at, the way the VCs look at it.
3. Narrow your list still further by zeroing in on firms that show an interest in the industry sector you aim to enter. We'll discuss shortly how to find that out.

By identifying the firms that meet all three criteria, you will have narrowed your list down to a more manageable number.

Venture Capitalists' View of Deal Stages

In Chapter 4, in discussing how investors can find the venture capital firm most suitable to their needs and desires, we shared how venture capitalists categorize deal stages according to the National Venture Capital Association in its 2015 Yearbook. We'll repeat that briefly here, to make things easier for you than having to turn back to that chapter.

Seed Stage

This stage is when a relatively small amount of capital (generally less than $500,000 and rarely more than $1 million) is provided to an inventor or entrepreneur to prove a concept both technically and commercially. The money is generally used for product development and market research and, if the initial steps are successful, to build an initial management team and develop a business plan. This is generally a premarketing stage.

Early Stage

In this stage, financing is provided to companies completing product development, when products are mostly in testing or pilot production. In some cases, product may have just been made commercially available. Companies may be in the process of organizing or they may already be in business, generally for three years or less. Usually such firms will have completed market studies, assembled the key management team, and developed a business plan, and are ready to start or have already started conducting business.

Expansion Stage

Financing at this stage often involves providing working capital for the initial expansion of a company that is producing, shipping, and has growing inventories and accounts receivable. It may or may not be showing a profit. Some of the uses of capital may also include further plant expansion, marketing, or development of an improved product. Larger, institutional-oriented venture capital firms are more likely to be involved at this stage, along with investors from previous rounds.

Later Stage

Capital in this stage is provided for companies that have reached a more stable growth rate, not growing as fast as during the expansion stage. These companies may or may not be profitable, but are more likely to be than in previous stages. Companies at this stage may have reached positive cash flow, but seek additional funding to fuel further substantial growth, including companies considering IPO or other exit options.

Targeting Your Money Search Based on VC Industry Focus

Some venture capital firms differentiate themselves based on the industries in which they invest. They may invest in some predetermined range of strategic industries or perhaps even focus on just one or two. Some industries typically chosen for focus include information technology, telecommunications, mobile applications, big data, and biotechnology, to name just a few, industries where there's lots of market-changing innovation and major growth potential.

Targeting your money search based on VC firms' focus on your industry sector makes sense for a few reasons:

- It's what they are interested in. Why waste time soliciting firms that aren't interested in investing in your industry?
- They likely have substantial knowledge of and a well-developed network of expert resources in your industry.
- Their investors as well may also have expert knowledge and a network of contacts in your industry, and may even be able to help as informal champions of your company.

How to Do All This VC Screening

There are a number of lists and databases to help you through the previously suggested three-step screening. We covered much of this in Chapter 4, but re-present the highlights here for ease of reference for entrepreneurs.

FindTheCompany.com has the most complete database we're aware of, totaling around 1,200 firms, and their database can be accessed after a simple, free registration process. Their summary list shows firm location, the deal stages on which they focus, and each firm's minimum and maximum investments in any given deal. You can then drill down for each firm to a more substantial database showing numbers of deals they've done, the number of companies in their current portfolio, and specific portfolio companies and their industries. They even show for each firm the size of each of their investments, cumulative funds invested, and the scale of their exits and the nature of each exit (e.g., IPO or acquisition). Despite the extensity of their database, though, even this one is not complete, nor do we suspect any is, as it doesn't even include our existing firm or our new online firm despite a recent $1 billion+ exit for one of our portfolio companies that received considerable press.

WalkerSands Communications, a Chicago- and San Francisco–based public relations firm specializing in B2B tech companies, also offers a helpful list of venture capital firms serving tech startups (http://www.walkersands.com/Us-Venture-Capital-Firms-For-Tech-Startups). This database provides for each firm its location, deal stage focus, industry focus, total capital, and notable investments. It is not nearly as complete as FindTheCompany.com, though, providing information on only a little more than 100 firms, primarily larger firms, with about half those listed having capital of at least $1 billion.

Another helpful list can be found on the industry association's (National Venture Capital Association) website (www.nvca.org). Their database, which is more extensive than WalkerSands' but still substantially less comprehensive than FindTheCompany.com's, lists their nearly 350 member firms and provides links to the website of each individual member firm. Those individual firm websites generally provide all the data provided in the others' lists and even more. Again, however, this list is incomplete, including only member firms and so leaving out any of us (like our firms) that are not dues-paying members.

An Alternative: Introduction through Expert Middlemen

An alternative, and higher probability, way of capturing VC attention is via introduction through expert middlemen. Here you sell your idea to an investment banker, new business lawyer, accountant, business broker, or other middleman. The good ones have developed working relationships with a handful of venture capitalists.

If your plan is forwarded by a middleman who has a venture capitalist's confidence and attention, it is more likely to go to the head of the line, a big advantage considering the large numbers of plans and proposals that reach the venture capitalist. These middlemen are valuable individuals for the time-pressed venture capitalist and for you. They can be found most readily through referrals from other entrepreneurs who have been in your shoes before. They may also be reached through entrepreneurial/startup forums and related networking groups found in a number of major markets.

Once you have identified these key venture capital contacts/ middlemen, you'll want to interview them to learn about their past success (or lack thereof) in venture capital placements. Which VCs do they know, how well do they know them, how many deals have they done together, and how much money have they made or lost together? Importantly, you need a middleman who can open the door for you and then get out of the way and let you present and sell directly to the VC.

Making Contact with the VC

Before you reach out to the VC, you'll need to have your ducks in a reasonably tidy row. You need to be able to communicate your idea concisely and compellingly—the 20-second elevator pitch that quickly captures the VC's attention and interest. You'll also want to be able to provide a compelling presentation, perhaps 15 to 30 slides, that fleshes out the idea and communicates the special nature of your business opportunity, identifies your allies and competitors, explains how your business will make money and why it should be successful, and presents your management team and its credentials and relevant experience. Depending on the stage, you may or may not already have a detailed business plan plotting out your growth plan details, showing more explicitly how you're going to make money, how much money you intend to make and how fast, and projecting your cash flow and cash needs as you ramp up.

One way of approaching a venture capitalist, particularly if you don't have a middleman ally, could be to call and indicate that you would like to forward your plan, but first would like some expert counsel in completing the formal document. Ask if the VC could suggest individuals who might be able to help with that counsel. Rather than appearing deficient, you will likely be viewed as resourceful and action-oriented.

Another approach could be to call the VC, let him know you have a unique and compelling idea (this is where that 20-second elevator pitch comes in handy), and ask if you could meet to discuss the idea further and learn more about what is required to raise venture capital. Few VCs can resist such a direct appeal to their professional obligations, ego, and desire to give birth to (and gain substantial financial rewards from) a unique new idea. Of course, before you call, be sure to qualify your prospect through the three-step screening process explained earlier in this chapter.

A word of caution: Reaching the venture capitalist for that conversation can be frustrating. Some VCs travel extensively, and when they are in the office, their days can be filled with phone calls and meetings. Don't be put off by those direct phone contact misses and excuses you may hear. They are probably real. Be persistent—keep trying and leave word as to where and when you can be reached. If you reach an administrative assistant, get to know that person so you can enlist his or her support in reaching your target. If you reach only voicemail, keep your messages clear, concise, and positive; again, the 20-second elevator pitch could come in handy in speeding the VC's return call.

Other Ways of Making Contact

While reaching the VC directly for that individualized attention is obviously the goal, venture capital fairs and a range of related forums and gatherings also can provide an opportunity for you to expose your idea to venture capitalists, as well as to middlemen who can help you get to the VC. At many of these gatherings, the capital-seeking companies make brief presentations to the assembled venture capitalists. Then the VCs sign up for smaller individual meetings where the dialogue can proceed one-on-one.

Such venture capital fairs, featuring a variety of specific formats along similar general lines, are held in many major markets across the country. A simple Internet search will let you know about a number of them. You may feel like a lamb among wolves at some of these forums, but they do provide an excellent opportunity to compare your approach to capital formation relative to others seeking venture capital funds.

Venture incubators and accelerators also offer opportunity for practical learning that will help advance your venture, as well as providing exposure to angel investors, venture capitalists, and middlemen involved in the world of ventures. Again, a simple Internet search will help you identify such entities accessible to you.

A notable such integrated venture environment can be found right in our firm's Chicago backyard in an entity called 1871. Its name was inspired by the coming together of engineers, architects, and inventors in Chicago following the city's great fire of 1871 that killed over 300 people, destroyed roughly three square miles of the city, and left 100,000 people homeless.

Founded in 2012, 1871 was created to support Chicago's digital startup community. Since that time, it has become the hub for the city's thriving technology and entrepreneurial ecosystem. Today 1871 is the home of more than 400 early-stage, high-growth digital startups. It also offers numerous educational programs and hosts presentation fairs and pitch competitions well attended by the regional venture capital community.

Evolution of the Venture Capital Community: Angel Groups and Online VC Portals

As you plan your pursuit of investor dollars, you should also consider some recent developments and growing trends in the venture capital community that may be quite relevant to your early needs. This is particularly the case if you are in the seed or very early stages of developing your venture and your funding needs are limited, perhaps in the range of $500,000 or less.

One development, while not really new, that has grown in importance in recent years is angel investor groups. These are groups dedicated to providing seed funding for promising ventures whose needs have outgrown family and friends but whose dollar needs are not yet ready for most traditional VCs.

Angel investor groups generally consist of affluent "civilians"—accredited individual investors but not professional venture capitalists—who work together in finding and screening ventures and then pool their monies to invest in these ventures. They typically focus on ventures in their specific geography. While most these groups come together based simply on a shared interest in supporting innovative, high-potential startups, some reflect other shared affinities. For example, the authors' graduate school alma mater, the Harvard Business School, has spawned a number of geographically based angel investor groups among its alumni.

According to the Angel Capital Association, in 2014 angels invested $24 billion in support of 73,000 startups, an average of roughly $330,000 per startup. This contrasts with an average financing round in 2014 among traditional venture capital firms of $11 million—$50.3 billion invested across 4,412 deals, according to the *MoneyTree Report* from PricewaterhouseCoopers and the National Venture Capital Association. For perspective, our firm, which focuses on early-stage deals, primarily A round, seeks investment opportunities in the $500,000 to $5 million range. Later-stage rounds are typically much larger, as companies' funding needs grow to finance increased manufacturing capacity, expanded working capital, and heightened marketing efforts to speed market penetration.

The Angel Capital Association consists of over 240 groups. These are primarily angel groups, whose own members number over 13,000 individuals, but include as well a number of online venture capital investment platforms and also some family investment offices. The listing of member groups can be found at https://www.angelcapitalassociation.org/directory/.

More on Online Venture Capital Investment Platforms

A truly new development in venture capital is the recent emergence of the above-mentioned online venture capital investment portals.

These firms have increased significantly the accessibility of investment opportunity for the roughly ten million Americans who qualify as accredited investors. This in turn has increased accessibility of funds for entrepreneurs seeking venture capital funding.

These online firms actively invite entrepreneurs to seek funding from their investors. Some of these firms offer their investors dozens, and sometimes even a hundred or more, portfolio companies. Focus tends to be at the seed and early stages. Their investments in each company tend to average considerably less than $1 million, far less than more traditional venture capital firms and closer to what one might expect from an angel group. Some of these online equity crowdfunders even charge the entrepreneurs for the right to raise funds on their portals, so watch out!

A few of the leaders in this field include FundersClub, SeedInvest, and AngelList. These firms operate almost like venture shopping malls, bringing together potential investors with large numbers of ventures. They often fill the role of super-angel groups, serving as a conduit for experienced angel investors to build syndicates of individual investors on their sites.

These firms claim to perform substantial due diligence, and unquestionably some do, though we wonder about how much rigor is possible given the large numbers of portfolio companies offered. For perspective, our firm offers only four to eight deals per year, and reviews more than 100 ventures for every deal we offer. We also wonder how much value these new firms can add in helping to guide and mentor venture leaders, given the large number of ventures in their portfolios.

Nevertheless, for the entrepreneur whose money needs are more modest, this more accessible source of funding may work. However, of course, the presumed lesser degree of subsequent involvement with portfolio companies may reduce success odds for the entrepreneur. Because these firms are relatively new, it is too soon to demonstrate a meaningful track record in terms of successful exits for their investors and the entrepreneurs they are funding.

The latest new development on this horizon, which just began in mid-2016 with the issuance by the SEC of further enabling regulations (called Title III), is the ability for some of these firms to raise funds from non-accredited investors as well, whose net worth and income fall below accredited status thresholds set by the SEC. SeedInvest is such a firm, working with both accredited and non-accredited investors.

Restrictions on the size of investments from non-accredited investors are quite strict, though, which can result in needing large numbers of individual investors in order for the entrepreneur to raise the amount of funding he requires. We wonder about the administrative complications entrepreneurs may face in dealing with large numbers of less affluent and possibly less sophisticated investors. It is too early to know yet whether this will be a problem for entrepreneurs. In addition, the amount of dollars that can be raised by the entrepreneur within a year's period is also limited.

Despite these cumbersome regulations and restrictions, this new development does open up one more fundraising option for entrepreneurs. Perhaps these venture capital minor leagues may help more worthy entrepreneurs to get their ventures launched, demonstrate progress, and subsequently garner the greater support from more traditional VCs that will be needed to enable expansion, leading ultimately to a successful exit. Only time will tell.

9

The Final Exam: Due Diligence

Venture capitalists are both hunters and gatherers. They seek out the best and the brightest among entrepreneurs and their ideas. Once they have an initial intuition that they have found a likely winner, they go into data gathering and analysis mode, which in the industry is known as due diligence. All professional VC investment firms perform due diligence to some extent.

Is Due Diligence Really That Important?

How critical is due diligence to the probability of investment success? Since most VC investments fail, might rigorous due diligence be just a waste of time? Are there too many variables and chance events, particularly in a seed- or early-stage investment, for diligence to tilt the chances of success one way or another?

Some might argue that diligence doesn't really matter in the long run and that investment outcomes are mostly a function of luck. Isn't this much like what we've read in history books about Napoleon—that in order to win his battles, his biggest desire was for lucky marshals to lead his troops? There is little hard research evidence that the degree or competence of the diligence improves the number of wins for a VC firm. Even for many of the biggest and best-known VC firms, only about 15–20% of all their investments make any money at all, and lots fewer are home runs.

Does diligence help pick winners (or reduce the number of losers and the magnitude of their losses) or just provide false comfort for the naïve? Can an investor's rigorous diligence stack the odds so that her investments are more like a bet with the casino's proverbial "house odds"?

In our minds there is no question that due diligence definitely does matter—a lot. Those VC firms that year after year produce big returns do it at least in part because of superior due diligence. While they may also see better deals earlier and have the reputation to sign them up before others, it is their due diligence skill and discipline that enable them to recognize which ones are indeed better deals.

A Warning to Entrepreneurs: Beware of Limited Due Diligence

As an entrepreneur, you may wonder why we're stressing the importance of due diligence here with you rather than emphasizing this point in the first half of this book, which was directed more to investors. The answer is because a VC's commitment to solid due diligence should be important to the entrepreneur, too.

If you come across a firm that does very little due diligence, you should avoid working with them even if you're an entrepreneur who really needs funding. Try selling others instead. Firms that do little due diligence will have little credibility among their peers, whom they may need as co-investors with them. They may in fact be driven largely by the management fees they charge their investors (regardless of results)—or the fees that some of the equity crowdfunders even charge the entrepreneur—rather than being focused on achieving exceptional gains for their investors *and* for the entrepreneur by helping to build major companies.

Without solid due diligence, the investor may not understand what the entrepreneur is trying to accomplish, may not be able to evaluate the venture team's ability to execute, and may not know when and how to help the venture management team when the going gets tough, which it so often does.

Return on Due Diligence Investment Tough to Quantify

So what is the cost in time and effort to the entrepreneur seeking venture capital, and the return to the investor on the time and effort put into due diligence? Even though top-performing VCs will tell you that rigorous due diligence is essential, these can still be tough questions to answer, and the responses you get may differ substantially by constituency.

Consider the entrepreneur we heard at a seminar sponsored by a top-tier accounting firm, who described recently going through a major venture capital "physical":

> On the plus side, if you're running the company right, due diligence underscores your credibility to potential VC investors. The VCs reason that you're likely to carry on business after you're funded the same way you were able to describe it before. On the negative side, you are burning up a lot of time and energy, often answering and preparing to answer the same questions over and over again as you may meet with many potential VCs prior to successful funding.

Make No Mistake: Due Diligence Is Important

We VCs are trustees for other people's money. VCs raise funds either from institutional sources, which are also trustees for other people's money, or from high-net-worth individual accredited investors, who take a dim view about losing their own money. So the VC's job demands care and a degree of caution while investing in inherently risky ventures. His or her clients expect achievement of some of the highest rates of return and multiples on funds invested of almost any investment asset class. Think about the VC's stress (and the investor's stress, too), as he or she commits substantial dollars, often without any real control, but still feels responsible for the ultimate outcome. If the entrepreneur doesn't really know the market and what he or she is doing, or hasn't considered and planned for the venture's major risks, it is easy for all to be lost.

The answer to this risk/reward stress dilemma is due diligence. This is a practical necessity and also a legal term for checking things out, for looking closely before leaping, and for being prudent before investing rather than having regrets the day after.

What Due Diligence Is All About

VCs usually ask a lot of basic, and sometimes even seemingly dumb, questions. Those questions may sometimes seem worthy of a ten-year-old, yet that may be necessary in order to illuminate what the company and hence the VC's investment is all about and its chances of success.

Starting with a tabula rasa on a subject and asking questions that may seem worthy of a child but can also be illuminating is not child's play. This is serious and can be scary stuff. The VC image may be of a smart, sophisticated, knowledgeable, perhaps even artful, high-powered money-man, but behind that façade always lurks fear of the unknown and perhaps the unknowable.

At their core, the due diligence questions are basic: What does this venture or its product do? How does it work? Who will buy it? Why do they want it? How many can we sell? What's the cost to make it? Can it be scaled up? Will the dogs (customers) eat the dogfood? Who are these people who want to build a business? Why and how will they succeed against the odds? Will the competition kill them? Will they be good partners or, even if they succeed, not worth the aggravation?

Time and again, an effective venture capitalist must reveal ignorance. This is not a business for people who need to appear smart. The VC in the due diligence process is revealing vulnerability.

Of course, there is a sharp edge to this seeming vulnerability. The venture capitalist stills holds the gold, and the entrepreneur wants it. For the entrepreneur, after a while the questions may begin to grate and to annoy. The savvy entrepreneur, however, begins to realize that behind the seemingly benign questions is a loaded and essential purpose. The venture capitalist is probing for both strengths and weaknesses, looking for the home run deal while probing for the tragic flaw and for any red flags as to why *not* to invest.

The Due Diligence Process

The due diligence process is rather straightforward. The venture capitalist will call several weeks after an office introductory meeting and say that it is time to do some additional homework on your deal. He'll tell you he will be in your area on a particular date and will ask if you and the key members of your team can make a tire-kicking meeting. Unless it's absolutely impossible, cancel all your other meetings and don't appear to have a full calendar. You need the money, and one of the first venture capital screens is a measure of your availability to the VC and your attitude about having an investment partner. The VC is signaling that he may invest in you and in return wants your full time and attention.

Once the initial diligence meeting has been set, the entrepreneur should be certain that other key managers are also available for the meeting. It's frustrating for a VC to arrive at the entrepreneur's place of business and find that the marketing VP is on the road selling or the product development VP is attending a design meeting. Common business courtesy requires that the entire senior management team is ready and available. Such courtesy is an important signal to the VC. If you treat the VC with such courtesy appropriate to his need, he is likely to conclude that you will do the same for your other critical customers as well.

After appropriate introductions are out of the way, including getting to know the history and backgrounds of your key team members, the VC may want a tour of your facilities if there are any of significance. Alternatively, he may begin to discuss with the team key elements of the company's business plan, presentation deck, elevator pitch, or bumper-sticker slogan.

An experienced VC can sense much from this early part of the diligence process and begin to form a picture as to the merits of an investment. At this juncture, integrating his pre-meeting background homework with his initial observations from this meeting, he will have some view as to how you fit into the industry universe, how likely it is that you can capture a very large market share quickly, and whether you have a handle on a rapid go-to-market strategy.

VCs, of course, come from various backgrounds. Some have managed plants; some are most comfortable with balance sheets; some focus mostly on the people. During the prelude to the tour, the entrepreneur will probably focus mostly on the people. Before beginning the tour, the entrepreneur and her team should also learn enough about the VC's needs and interests to tailor communications most effectively. The ability to learn quickly about the VC's needs and interests can signal the venture team's ability to listen, a critical skill since they need to be able to listen effectively to customers as well in order to better understand and address their needs.

As the entrepreneur conducting a facility or plant tour, it's important to highlight the venture's strengths, pertaining both to people and to physical assets. Be sure introductions are made to other key employees on the tour and that a feel is provided for the focus and chemistry of the business organization. This is also an ideal time to inspect and demonstrate, if possible, an engineering or production prototype of your product. You can point out the interesting features of your product, engineering, and sales and marketing processes that enhance your uniqueness as an investment opportunity. You can show how the device or service works in real time.

Time is often relatively short in this initial due diligence meeting—perhaps a half-day—so concentrate on the informative and dramatic in this initial tour. Show the venture capitalist what you have that others will want to buy and why major money will be made.

Of course, the facility tour is not only an opportunity to judge product or market uniqueness. It is also an opportunity to show the venture capitalist what you have that others will want to buy and why major growth in revenue and profit will occur, and to begin to outline the likely growth evolution of the business. The VC is attempting to gauge just how fast the company can scale revenue and move to positive cash flow and profitability, especially if those are near-term goals.

After the facility tour, the venture capitalist will often want to quiz the management team on their business plans. Some of the questions will be very basic, but others will be very specific, getting into market, competition, forecasts, and financial projections, as well as other subjects.

The Focus of Due Diligence Questioning

Generally the earlier the deal stage—such as seed, startup, or a Series A investment—the more the questions will be about management and their capabilities. For an early-stage investment, the jockey (i.e., founder and management team) is often more critical, and so less emphasis is placed on the horse (the specific business/market opportunity and projected details). The later the deal stage, the more the questions will be about margins, growth rates, scaling, and time to positive cash flow and profitability.

Often in an early-stage investment, the management team is not fully complete. There is a jockey, the founding entrepreneur, but the company is short on the groomers, stable hands, track workers, and so on. Prior to seeking venture capital, the entrepreneur should analyze the management team's soft spots and develop a plan to fill the gaps. Potential new members of the team may not want their identity disclosed prior to venture capital funding, as the venture may not yet be able to pay them for their efforts or may falter for lack of funding prior to liftoff. Nevertheless, the lead jockey/founding entrepreneur may be able to provide sufficient information on targeted recruits' prior experience to convince the VC that a complete management team is on the horizon.

Experienced VCs, of course, look for both a good horse and a good jockey. The earlier the stage, though, the more management is critical, as the VC is particularly interested in management's ability to make the initial reference sales that launch the company as a real business rather than just an idea. In the early-stage deal, the VC will want to understand the uses of the capital invested. Often at this stage, the major use is to begin to implement a go-to-market sales strategy, so this strategy will be closely scrutinized.

In a later-stage company, where there are more hard assets as well as hard or soft liabilities, the venture capitalist will want to understand their placement and deployment in support of the company's strategy, as well as how effective and efficient the company has been with previous capital invested. The VC will be attempting to judge if the company will need more investment capital as well as both the upside opportunities and downside risks for the investment. The VC is particularly interested in the downside risks for soft-asset companies such as those selling software (which, in the memorable phrase of iconic VC Mark Andreessen, may both eat the world and also eat the company). The VC must be particularly diligent where the product or software as a service (SaaS) can easily walk out the door with the proprietor.

Judgments will be made as to whether the entrepreneur is a business realist or a dreamer, and whether she has sufficient hands-on experience and knowledge of the industry and market to succeed. The venture capitalist is not in the business of providing the entrepreneur with a business education; since venture capital is one of the last refuges of the business generalist, the venture capitalist will want the entrepreneur to demonstrate the specific knowledge and skills required to succeed in the highly specific marketplace.

The price the VC will be willing to pay with his investment, and the terms on which the VC may be willing to invest, will be strongly influenced by his impressions and conclusions from this inspection tour and evaluation. This is not a time to withhold and be wary. The VC is not in the business of stealing others' business ideas or products. In such a still relatively small and highly networked industry, poaching behavior would soon result in being out of business. Provide full disclosure and treat the VC like a trusted partner.

Importance of Treating the VC with Respect and Sincerity

One of the worst feelings a VC can have is when the entrepreneur forgets the VC's name after the money is in the deal. This sometimes occurs when the entrepreneur really didn't view the VC as a helpful partner; the entrepreneur wanted no-strings money so that he could continue to build his business in his own way without outside governance contributions or management interference.

Since entrepreneurs are often very independent and resourceful, some have the attitude that they can do it all without any support other than capital. This go-it-alone attitude is fine if you really can go-it-alone, but it can be perilous for an entrepreneur who raises venture capital, as that entrepreneur will almost certainly need to go back to the VC for *something*, whether additional capital, customer references, a pat on the back, or having the entrepreneur's back in tough times. Once a VC realizes that the entrepreneur doesn't want to act as a real partner, trouble begins. As long as a VC has money invested, he needs to be treated like the entrepreneur's best customer.

When America Online, after its escape from near-early-death, was restaged, management of the investors was accorded high priority and tended to wholeheartedly by Jim Kimsey, the new chairman and CEO. As a former restaurant and bar owner, among other talents, Kimsey knew that the VC investors—and there were several of them—were his best customers. He recognized that he would need more of their money and lots of their patience and faith. Jim knew how to "get them the best table, a cold drink, and a good pour."

While he saw to the care and feeding of the VC investors, Marketing VP Steve Case was freed up to concentrate on product development, the marketing message, and initial customer acquisition. The inside/outside team of Kimsey and Case made America Online happen. The investors included many of America's major VC firms, and careful handling of their needs and interests was critical, particularly for a company that had come so close to death and had to be so fully restaged.

Some entrepreneurs believe that it is most effective, when "whetting the venture capitalist's appetite," to appear relatively aloof and in no real need of funds during this due diligence process, often dropping subtle hints that there are many others interested in the opportunity and that the VC must move fast to make an investment. This may work with the newer recruits to the industry or with the desperate VC who may then be inclined to pay up a bit for the investment, but in the long run the relationship will suffer. The VC is in a position generally to get even in later-round investments if he believes he has paid too much, too soon, or that he has not really had full disclosure.

In the discussions with the VC, it is best for the founding entrepreneur to avoid appearing as if walking on water is one of the skills perfected. The venture capitalist is looking to back those entrepreneurs who have solid self-confidence but not too much arrogance. The late Pat Lyles, a legendary Harvard Business School instructor and a general partner at early Boston-based VC partnership Charles River, said, "I want to invest with 'I want to do well' egos rather than with those that are essentially delusional over their self-importance."

While a swelled head is not normally helpful to fundraising, the venture capitalist will want to deduce through due diligence that the entrepreneur is a visionary with a compelling dream, a big thinker. As VCs have in recent years become more interested in home run investments, a big thinker with a perceived opportunity to build a multimillion-dollar, if not a billion-dollar, business (the so-called unicorns because they are so rare) has become essential. While spinning the dream, though, it is also important that the entrepreneur be grounded in the here and now, in the world of fast execution.

It's also helpful to convey that the founder sincerely wants to be very rich. The VC's search and due diligence efforts are not to find ego-driven empire builders, but rather to find and qualify certifiable moneymakers. There's certainly nothing wrong with the modern mantra of wanting to save or change the world, but the VC recognizes that the world is hard to change and even harder to save. A number of VCs will not invest in projects that they view as detrimental to society but, in the end, they are judged on their ability to produce returns that outperform almost all other types of investment. So, as long as the investment does no harm, it really is mostly about the money.

Time Can Be of the Essence

For a VC investor pursuing a high-quality investment opportunity, there is often not much time to conduct due diligence. If the opportunity is a good one, then there will often be many suitors and all will be driving fast toward the hoop. In these rapid-fire circumstances, the only way to win is not to reduce the quality of the diligence, but rather for the VC to find opportunities before others so that he has a head start on other competitive investors, and for the VC to focus diligence efforts smartly on those areas that are most important.

As explained before, for a seed, startup, or early-stage investment, much of the due diligence effort should be focused on getting to know well and understand the jockey and the team. For a later-stage investment, the execution ability of the team will often already have been demonstrated, so the main question will be whether the team has a viable plan to scale up the opportunity toward a successful exit.

Recently, a Chicago-based company in digital mass storage and security called Cleversafe was sold to IBM for $1.3 billion, one of the largest (if not the very largest) tech unicorn exits in Chicago venture capital history. The exit created over 80 millionaires, many from Chicago, including a number of Cleversafe employees, who are now reinvesting their gains in other Chicago-based companies.

Early Series A investors in Cleversafe did not have much time to make their investment decision. Our firm, Batterson Venture Capital, had heard about the company through several respected network contacts, and we then attended a tech conference where the company's founder, Chris Gladwin, presented. Gladwin's presentation laid out a compelling case that his unique idea—to split up data into slices, send the data slices for storage over the cloud to a number of silos, and then in real time reassemble the data using a proprietary algorithm—presented the opportunity to both significantly lower the cost of big data storage (by up to 80%) and improve data security. Gladwin had also founded several earlier companies that did well, so his ability to assemble a team and execute was also clear and compelling.

Essentially the decision to invest was made during Gladwin's tech conference presentation. Due diligence follow-up on the analytical issues was handled very rapidly soon after. A highly experienced venture capitalist can make these decisions quite rapidly. Less experienced VCs would normally be better served finding investment opportunities where time is not so much of the essence, perhaps even letting go of some of what may appear to be the highest value opportunities.

Some Advice for Less Experienced VCs

For those who are just beginning to invest in or have limited experience in venture capital, allowing sufficient time for diligence is particularly important to help reduce the number of losing investments and the magnitude of the losses, even though this may also reduce the number of major winners. In the beginning, reducing losses, rather than winning big, may be more important in keeping a new VC in the game. (Studies have shown that there is much more pain in losing than pleasure in winning.) So taking the time for necessary diligence to avoid losing is a winning strategy.

The more experienced VC (it is said that it takes a minimum of $15 million in losses to train a VC) can assume more risk by moving faster. This investor will be better able to recognize pretty much right away which potential investments are more likely to lose or to win. The ideal approach is to both have high-quality deal flow (and also to create it through developed networks and reputation) as well as undertake extensive diligence, the amount depending on the level of experience.

Even with the best diligence and intentions, it is often said, "A VC only really learns the actual state of affairs at the first company board meeting." VC investing is an ongoing learning process about the venture team, the industry, the markets, the products, and the competition. As information increases and the company progresses through existing investments, the VC usually is able to make additional investments in the company based on this additional hard-won knowledge.

In the end, diligence does matter, whether it is facilitated and accelerated by deep experience or more reliant on a deep and more time-consuming dive into facts, as most VCs will invest in only about one out of a hundred companies that come to them, with perhaps five to ten out of the hundred going through diligence. The process of deal flow screening and due diligence in essence consists of (1) elimination of the lame, then (2) elimination of those who can only walk well, and then (3) investing in those that can run like a true winning athlete.

Some Advice for Less Experienced Investors

Working and/or investing at first with experienced investors will best serve the individual new to the game. Since it is very difficult for individuals to gain access to major institutional venture capital funds with long successful track records, an effective alternative approach is to seek out opportunity to invest with experienced individual investors or to rely on a venture capital firm with a proven track record that is accessible to individuals.

In recent years, new avenues for investment with the best and brightest individuals have been created, in particular through readily accessible online VC investment firms. One example is AngelList, which offers the chance to invest alongside and with investors who have successful track records as entrepreneurs and/or investors. These individuals do the work of a VC in finding deal opportunities and doing the due diligence homework and then form *syndicates* including other investors who may have less experience.

Other significant online VCs offering individual investors dozens of deals include FundersClub, CircleUp, SeedInvest, and Israel-based OurCrowd. These emerging online VC investment firms offer the new investor the opportunity to co-invest with experienced investors and to piggyback on the knowledge networks and diligence of qualified venture capital investors, so they may achieve something closer to playing with house odds rather than against the house. The chances should be better than investing with a brother-in-law or the local angel group breakfast investment club.

A word of caution: With many of these firms offering such a large number of deals, the buyer should beware, as the quality of the deals, the ability of the syndicator in the case of AngelList, and the level of diligence can vary widely. Doing 40 or so deals a year, like some of these firms do, requires a strong due diligence focus and substantial due diligence resources to do this job well. It is not yet clear if such a model will work in the end, as VC investment models over the years have had difficulty scaling from smaller boutique firms with several partners to larger organizations doing lots more deals.

In addition, while these VC firms have raised considerable capital both for the firms and their individual investment deals, these firms are so new that few of their investments have yet exited. Moreover, many of their deals are seed investments that will require considerable additional capital. Hence, only time will tell if their models will be successful.

VCapital is a new online VC investment firm, formed by the authors and their associates, which has distinct credentials and a distinct approach among these readily accessible online VC investment firms. The VCapital team leadership has about 35 years of highly successful venture capital investing experience, delivering an average annual gross IRR over that period of 28% and returning 3.6× the amount of funds invested. For perspective, 3× is considered an excellent return multiple. Over those 35 years, the team has never had a negative-returning fund, with average annual returns ranging from 14% to 159%. It has participated in early investments in three companies that reached market capitalizations of over $1 billion. This includes helping to found and create America Online (AOL), which was part of the largest company merger ever (AOL–Time Warner) and which was valued at the time of the merger at $364 billion. The $1 million investment made by the VCapital founder (Len) would have been valued in 1999, just before the merger, at $4.6 billion.

As with the team's predecessor firms, VCapital is highly selective in its deal selection, seeking just four to eight high-quality deals per year. It focuses about half its deals in the underserved Midwest region of the United States (and half in other areas of the country), where less intense VC competition than in places like Silicon Valley results in lower valuations/share prices for high-quality investments.

VCapital team members have previously either created as entrepreneurs or worked with entrepreneurs very closely to create new business opportunities. This means that investment opportunities will be well understood, and deals we actually pursue will be followed closely and knowledgably, increasing the odds of success. Net, the VCapital team is throwing its investment darts more selectively and with a surer aim, rather than "throwing darts in the dark" (or with less knowledge, experience, and/or due diligence).

Considering all this, our advice to new venture capital investors is that you "look as far as the eye can see, and know all the wonder that will be," but also remember to look hard before you leap. Falling repeatedly into the cavern of big losses can be awfully painful.

10

Finding Your Deal-Doing Lawyer

Your supporting player in the venture capital negotiating process should be a lawyer who knows how to say yes as well as no—the rare deal-doing lawyer.

So Many Types of Lawyers to Consider

There are a lot of different types of lawyers plying their craft. Consider all these different specializations and niches.

There are lawyers who specialize in personal injury litigation. There are real estate lawyers who are effective in anything from a house closing to setting up a real estate limited partnership syndication. There are labor lawyers who can handle anything from an age discrimination case to an appearance before the National Labor Relations Board.

There are lawyers who specialize in going to court, and there are those who are best at keeping you out of court. There are numerous branches of business lawyers—some who are best with large corporations; others are specialists before the Securities and Exchange Commission; a few are tax experts and will assist you in paying less and retaining more of your income.

There are now online legal firms where you fill out pre-prepared legal documents and effectively serve as your own lawyer. There are cut-rate lawyers who farm out work to attorneys working out of a closet rather than from fancy downtown offices. There are lawyers who no longer charge by the sacrosanct billable hour and will charge a fixed fee on a given job.

There are lawyers who know how to use the latest document analysis software to rapidly sort through massive numbers of documents and cut costs through automation. Artificial intelligence software is coming soon, which will analyze the documents, facts, and law and guide the lawyer toward a better, faster analysis at lower cost.

Why You Need a Deal-Doing Lawyer

For venture capital legal work, an entrepreneur needs a lawyer who knows how to say "yes" or "yes, but." These are the deal-doing lawyers, and they are rare and hard to find. Too many lawyers just know how to say "no."

Legal training teaches its future practitioners to think of the worst possible case or result that may befall a client and then to advise the client of the numerous disastrous ramifications that may occur. Since there are more things that can go wrong than go right, in business and in life in general, this focus on the downside is often not a bad idea. It certainly can result in more billable hours; and it is what a client is often quite willing to pay for—either to stay out of legal trouble or to get out of it.

In law school, this is known as the "cloud of fat caution." One of the authors (Len) remembers this well, as a graduate of the Washington University School of Law. Many lawyers are great examples of the principle of fat caution. This trait makes it constitutionally impossible for the majority of lawyers to see or believe in the positive side of much of anything. Given human nature and their exposure in their practices so often to the downside of the human equation, this pessimistic view isn't surprising.

An entrepreneur, on the other hand, by nature is an optimist, hopefully a realistic optimist, who tends to see mostly the sunny side rather than the dark side where most lawyers live. An entrepreneur is creating or pushing assets forward; most attorneys are holding them in check.

An entrepreneur needs a deal-doing lawyer who understands business and how it functions as well as being able to apply the law to business decisions. The best of these are not just lawyers, but also trusted business advisors who can counsel on business decisions as well as on their legal implications. They are able to protect interests while not inserting a negative bias or getting in the way of getting the deal done.

Knowledge of the Venture Capital Process

This attorney must also be familiar with the venture capital process, not the friend of a friend who helped with a recent house closing. Familiarity with the venture capital business and legal process means that a number of issues that would concern a less experienced, more pessimistic attorney will be understood in the right light by the deal-doing attorney and dismissed before they become a federal case.

If an attorney is really good, he or she will have the skill, experience, and even creativity in coming up with business/legal solutions that help bridge the gaps over the inevitable points on which the parties may disagree. If the major points are discovered early on, well prior to the closing, this helps eliminate the potential shootouts between the entrepreneur and venture investor that might otherwise emerge just prior to the closing.

Some Realities to Consider

An important question in any venture capital funding transaction is, do the documents really matter much? By the time funds change hands, the relationship between the venture capitalist and the entrepreneur should be one of trust and confidence, where a handshake should seem sufficient rather than needing reams of paper.

If the entrepreneur goes nowhere positive with the funds, rather than deploying them wisely to build the business, the venture capitalist, who is generally a minority investor, will be mostly out of luck regardless of the documents. If the entrepreneur treats the venture capitalist in an arm's-length legal way and does not act like a true partner, it is quite likely, in the next inevitable round of funding, that the venture capitalist will not act like a trusting partner, either, and will extract a pound of flesh. A good deal-doing lawyer understands this dynamic. While good fences may make good neighbors, in a venture capital financing, open gates should also be a feature.

Finding the Right Legal Counsel

Most major cities now have a number of experienced venture capital lawyers. The large cities with extensive venture capital support infrastructures tend to have the more prominent and experienced venture capital practitioners, and an appropriate reference from the venture capitalist will be likely to get their interest and attention.

For those entrepreneurs working in smaller cities or towns, their local attorney, banker, broker, or accountant can often be a good reference source. For those entrepreneurs who do not have the luxury of being located in an area with highly experienced venture capital counsel, the choice may be to find good local counsel with the desired characteristics who is interested in developing into a venture capital counsel. That attorney may in turn support his work by seeking advice and assistance from a more experienced out-of-town firm. It is common legal practice on many matters for the law firm that gets the business to farm out work in which it lacks real experience to a more experienced firm that specializes in venture capital financing.

Whatever firm the entrepreneur chooses, it's critical that the principal attorney who is retained will actually do the work on the deal, or will at least exercise close supervision over less experienced colleagues when she delegates work. One issue with a large firm is that the principal "rainmaker" attorney who brings in the business often delegates the actual legal work to another member of the firm, who then delegates to another, and so on. This legal team then often bills the client for the many communications among the team members as well as for the individual work of the attorneys, resulting in a big bill. Teams also often expand, adding other specialized members in employment law, tax, securities, and other areas. In addition, the larger the team, the more chance for miscommunication among the attorneys themselves. A good firm is as good at managing their attorney teams as they are in doing the actual legal work.

One more important consideration is to be certain that the selected attorney or firm will be readily available to close on the funding once essential business points have been agreed upon.

Speed Can Be Important

The business and emotional climate surrounding a venture capital deal can alter rapidly while waiting for your attorney to draft documents, so it's critical to have an attorney who can move the agreements along rapidly once the essential business points have been agreed on. If an overly protective attorney is engaged, or one who is not familiar with the venture capital scene, he can lawyer the deal to death and take forever to complete the work, while the venture capitalist stews.

The effective venture capital lawyer knows what points are critical, what points can be easily dispensed with, and what points may be worth hard negotiation. He also knows that once the legal documentation is completed and the deal closed, the legal papers will be filed, in most cases rarely to be opened again, and that the ongoing relationship between the venture capitalist and the entrepreneur will be far more important than his handiwork. He should work at all times to keep this relationship amicable and positive.

Lots of Legal Consistency

Generally the key points in a venture capital document are what is known in the trade as "legal boilerplate." Most of the provisions in the documents are very similar from deal to deal, differing only somewhat depending on the maturity of the company, its previous capital structure, the amount of capital invested, and the number of investors and attorneys involved in the transaction. The more attorneys, the more complex the documentation is likely to be, as each attorney will feel compelled to make some contribution to the overall result, to either keep the client happy that his interests are being protected or justify a fee.

In our experience, over the course of hundreds of venture capital investments and closings, rarely are the documents later consulted. The main reason for this lack of need to revisit them is that most venture capital investments either lose all the money or do well. Where the outcome is so clear, the documents do not normally come into play. An important exception to this is when there are numerous rounds of financing, with a large number of investors, a complex capitalization structure, and perhaps a number of payout preferences with waterfall provisions (i.e., detailing who gets what distributions in what order and amounts.)

Build Trust, Not Litigation

By and large, the venture capital community prefers at all cost to stay out of court. Besides being bad for future business, once a venture deal winds up in court, the venture capitalist will generally lose or will have already lost the investment capital.

Particularly fragile startups (which most are) simply will not normally survive serious acrimony and lawsuits. In a business of trust, once trust is broken, there are few pieces to pick up. Venture capitalists want to be the entrepreneur's partner, not litigant.

The Typical Process

Normally the lawyers for the venture capitalist will draw up the first draft of the required legal documents. The money is coming from the venture capitalist, so it is generally best to let the venture capital attorney start the process. While this may provide some slight negotiating advantage, that can be outweighed by the trust that can be engendered through the entrepreneur's professional deference to the venture capitalist. Once the entrepreneur receives the draft documents, they should then be reviewed and sent to the entrepreneur's attorney for his review and input.

There are a number of fairly standard venture capital documents with which it will help to be familiar. These documents will vary in both form and substance depending on the nature of the business deal. There are a number of guidebooks that list these documents and clearly explain their provisions and impact.

Generally, if the venture capitalist believes that he has been fair or generous on price, he may insist on a tougher document or instrument to protect him on the downside. Also, if the venture capitalist views the risk in the deal as being unusually high, he is likely to insist on additional protection in the majority of cases. This approach is not unusual and should be expected and respected. The late Stan Golder, of then Golder, Thomas, and Cressy, one of the most successful and most experienced venture capitalists, would say: "You name the price, and I will name the terms; you name the terms, and I will name the price." Continue to keep firmly in mind that the venture capitalist is continuously balancing mentally his risk and reward, and attempting to make on-the-fly adjustments based on these perceptions.

The lawyer for the venture capitalist will take the term sheet (outline of the major terms), which was negotiated and agreed upon between the company and the venture capital firm or firms, and will review its provisions to determine whether the terms are clear, understood by both parties, and complete. On some occasions, it is considered necessary by counsel, particularly in a more complex deal, to redraft the term sheet so that there is a real meeting of the minds that can be expressed and replicated in legal terms. This exercise, while time-consuming, can be useful in those deals that break new ground as to structure and terms.

If the deal is relatively straightforward, a redraft of the terms may not be necessary and may just be a way for the attorney to run up the bill. Most law firms do still bill on an hourly rate. The entrepreneur, if she is paying this bill for work done by the VC's lawyer, should feel free to request that the venture capitalist ask his law firm for an estimate of the billable hours, and should be alert, as the documentation proceeds, for excessive lawyering. Generally, however, the venture capitalists will pay their own legal bills, and the entrepreneur will pay the bill from her counsel.

The principal venture capital document is the stock purchase agreement, which comes in several colors and shades. Normally venture capitalists will want to purchase either common stock or, more often than not, a form of convertible security with some of the attributes of common stock and some aspects of the potentially more secure preferred stock issue. Essentially the venture capitalist is trying for the best of both worlds, the liquidity of common stock coupled with the security provisions and liquidation preferences (i.e., who gets paid first) of preferred stock. The stock purchase agreement will cover such items as the major terms determining price, type of security, use of proceeds, board of directors composition, registration rights, financial statements, anti-dilution protection, and various representations and warranties, such as that all taxes have been paid to date, the company is not in default, compliance with all laws, and so forth.

Differing Degrees of Legal Orientation

Some venture capital firms have more of a legal orientation to their deals and require more from the entrepreneur in the way of documentation and disclosure. The disclosure of key information can be highly important so that the venture capitalist is not surprised by negative information at the first board meeting.

Like most things in business, it is best to keep all of this as simple as the lawyers will allow. Finding the lawyer who can and will keep it all as simple and straightforward as possible, without extensive and expensive redrafting, can be key to legal peace of mind.

The attorney for the lead investor in a syndicate should take the lead gathering all syndicate members' legal comments and presenting them to entrepreneur's counsel. On occasion, if the entrepreneur is dealing with a large venture capital institution such as a corporate venture capital group, the entrepreneur will face both the VC's inside and outside counsel. The inside counsel will normally act as the legal coordinator and run interference for the outside counsel, who may actually sort out and advise on most major issues.

Occasionally, an entrepreneur will get his ego involved with the legal process itself and attempt to win the legal points. With legal issues, just as with business issues, it's best when a win/win between the entrepreneur and venture capitalist can be achieved. Legal documentation time is not the time to be scoring points, but rather to get the deal done correctly, completely, and carefully. Then, after that is accomplished, the objective is to have a continuing relationship that will work once the documents are put away and most often forgotten.

11

Financing Has Arrived and "You're Married" ... Now What?

After considerable effort and even greater stress, the entrepreneur has successfully prospected for potential investors, thrown her best pitches, negotiated carefully, and closed on a round of venture capital financing. The documents are put away. The entrepreneur is recovering from the late-night staff party celebrating both solvency and living another day. The check has cleared, the lawyers have been paid, and outstanding payables and back bills have been cleared up, paying off not only impatient creditors, but also the more patient and trusting ones. For the moment, immediate cash flow problems are in the rearview mirror.

Don't get too comfortable. The real work is now just beginning—building the company, as well as keeping the newly won, most important customers, the venture capitalist investors, content.

Now You Answer to a Higher Authority—a Board of Directors

The agreement you've just struck with the venture capitalists generally requires a formal board of directors if the company has not yet established one, or may call for changes in the composition of an already-existing board. A well-prepared entrepreneur will likely have a board in place even before the venture capital financing. Such a board often includes the technical founder, the chief executive officer, a director with strong industry experience in the company's major domain, and perhaps an attorney.

Generally the first-round venture capital investors will want to add at least one and perhaps two new directors of their choice. They will provide directors who can both contribute something new to the development of the company, often including valuable sales and industry contacts, and represent the interests of the venture capital investors. As additional financings are undertaken, the venture capitalists may want additional directors who also represent their interests.

For an early-stage company, a board of five is about right. Typically two are from management, two represent the venture capitalists, and there's one independent, industry-expert director. Any larger is likely to make communications and decision-making more difficult, often winding up with one autocrat dominating decisions rather than the more collaborative board that has been shown to add greater value.

The decisions that go into pulling together the new board can be difficult for the entrepreneur. In the case of companies that already had a functioning board, it is often necessary to move aside existing directors who have been loyal supporters through the first tough days.

If there are too many VCs on the board (or even attending as observers without voting rights), too much of the board meetings will often be taken up with sorting out the considerable venture capitalist egos around the table. The first half-hour of many meetings can be taken up simply with coordinating the VCs' travel schedules for the next meeting date, despite some really good meeting-planning software available at little cost. A friendly suggestion: Plan to set the meetings for an entire year well ahead of time, and don't let one VC try to trump another over meeting times and places.

Be Ready to Make Management Changes

An early-stage company that is undergoing rapid growth, or that aspires to grow revenues by 100% or more per year, evolves through many distinct stages very rapidly. It may evolve in three to five years through all the stages a more normal growth company would experience over 10 to 20 years.

In the more leisurely business development cycle, typical attrition and normal growth-driven organizational changes resolve many of the personnel—and more personal—issues. The fast-growing, venture capital–supported company, on the other hand, will be faced with personnel issues requiring more immediate decisions. It's important, therefore, to have employment and severance contracts with key employees that will cover rapid changes in employee responsibilities as well as govern matters of retention or termination.

One early management change the venture capital group is likely to push for immediately following a venture capital financing is the addition of a qualified chief financial officer (CFO). Such a management addition may be absolutely necessary if the financing agreement calls for an official audit. It's nearly impossible to conduct a sound audit without the expertise of a CFO who has been down this road before.

On the other hand, one personnel task where the venture capital-supported entrepreneur can save time is succession planning. Generally in a VC-backed company, there is little if any succession planning, as the goal is to exit prior to this becoming an issue. Further, staffing should be lean and the management bench not very deep. Moreover, many VC-backed companies fail early, so succession planning never comes into play.

Anticipate Complications and Management Challenges

As with most aspects of life, a change in one place often leads to ripples of change elsewhere. The entrepreneur's challenge in managing a rapidly evolving business organization is no different. You need to anticipate and plan for those rippling effects. You won't have the luxury of your own measured learning or of a nurturing employee corporate development program. You will need to get accustomed to perceiving and addressing those rippling effects while learning on-the-fly.

Our experience is that it is generally best to have strong, explicit responsibility and process boundaries and that all employees know clearly their roles in the company. Without these boundaries, chaos can quickly result. Early-stage venture teams are often composed of highly aggressive, entrepreneurial individuals who, left to their own devices, may instinctively attempt to take on responsibilities belonging to other team members. The results are predictable—strife and confusion.

As team leader, the entrepreneur must anticipate such complications and sort out essential readjustments quickly, before the friction leads to organizational fire. The entrepreneur is the fire marshal. The entrepreneur also needs to be vigilant to ebbs and flows of employee motivation and productivity. Some employees may start like a house-a-fire but then flame out, while others may start more slowly but then burn brightly at the steady pace the organization needs.

The Critical Search for Talent as the Venture Evolves

An essential ingredient in building the venture toward the hoped-for wealth-creating outcome is finding and recruiting the key employees needed as the venture evolves. This isn't easy, but it is vitally important.

Several alternative recruiting methods are possible and should be considered. These include the use of executive search recruiters, assistance from the venture capital investors (remember the importance of not only their *know-how*, but also their *know-who*), referrals by the board of directors, and running ads on Internet job search sites, which are now numerous and can be effective. Don't sell short the potential walk-in candidate who seeks you out. That instinctive entrepreneurial bent may prove highly compatible with and valuable in an environment where being a self-starter is key to success and advancement.

Any of these methods can be effective as long as the entrepreneur, ideally with the advice and consent of the board, venture investors, and existing key employees, has carefully reviewed the requirements of the job, identified the prerequisites that should maximize probability of success, and determined what type of personality would be a fit for the emerging company culture and the entrepreneur's style.

The need for speed and cost efficiency often pushes the entrepreneur to lower cost search methods. For example, after working up and reviewing specifications for the job with the VCs and the board, he may ask the venture capital investors or board members if they know anyone who may be qualified for the particular position. Venture capitalists receive a number of resumes from job-seekers each week, and on occasion one of these may be a good fit with a portfolio company's needs.

Another potential low-cost search method is to contact alumni placement offices of leading business schools and universities that maintain lists and information on alumni seeking new challenges to conquer. If you are not yourself an alumna or alumnus of a school that might be a fertile hunting ground (and you may need to be one in order to access the list and/or the placement office's help), the entrepreneur is likely to know one who can secure such access. Still another very low-cost option to find interested candidates who may meet your needs is the use of LinkedIn. In addition, while we earlier mentioned the electronic job board sites, more traditional newspaper ads, such as those in the *Wall Street Journal*, while perhaps a longer shot for a good fit, can attract qualified candidates and may work.

Executive Search Consultants: Expensive, But Can Be Worth It

If you've never had experience with a qualified executive search consultant and assume they are simply too expensive, we urge you to keep an open mind. Generally their fee is a substantial portion, usually a third, of the hired executive's first-year salary. While this approach is admittedly not cheap, the selection of the right new management member can make a critical difference.

Also, a number of major executive search firms are interested these days in working with the venture capital–supported company, as entrepreneurship has become all the rage, and they may be willing to work with you on the cost side. They reason that, for the venture capital–supported company, the probability of at least some degree of success is great enough that eventually, assuming a positive relationship is established, they will realize greater financial returns. Some will even take their fee or a portion of it in company equity.

Use of an executive search firm may be especially worthwhile in the case of finding a new chief executive officer (CEO). CEOs are occasionally replaced, usually with the new one recruited from outside the company. This takes place generally either when the company has outgrown the existing CEO's skill set or when the company is in trouble and/or its growth has slowed.

Achieving the confidence of the board is critical for the founder/CEO. Without this confidence, the entrepreneur is not likely to remain CEO for an extended period. It's important for the CEO and her tenure that the relationship with each board member is one of full disclosure and that board members are consulted for their views on a regular basis regarding key decisions. It's not enough to rely on the work at regular board meetings alone.

Our Batterson Venture Capital firm's experience with a venture called Cleversafe is a wonderful illustration of how worthwhile retention of an executive search consultant can be in finding the right CEO to move the venture forward. We've already told you about this Chicago-based data storage company's recent sale to IBM for $1.3 billion. An important factor contributing to that home run exit was the retention of a recognized executive search firm, once the commercial potential of the company's disruptive new technology was confirmed through its success with a number of major early-adopter customers, to find a new CEO to build a more aggressive sales and marketing culture. The search, which was led on the company side by the Cleversafe chairman (who was also a major investor), former Motorola CEO Christopher Galvin, found John Morris, then with Jupiter Networks in Silicon Valley, and brought him to Chicago as CEO.

Morris had earlier been an IBM executive and knew the IBM culture and many of its executives as well. Within about two years, Morris had rapidly expanded Cleversafe sales, leading to its sale to IBM. Importantly, besides knowing the industry well, including IBM, the new CEO had to fit into the Cleversafe culture and also get along with the founder/former CEO and the board of directors, all while building the business for a major successful exit.

Galvin's selection of Morris was not just accidental luck. A few years earlier, Galvin had triggered a similar executive change at Navteq, a Chicago-based provider of geographic information systems and electronic navigable maps such as automotive navigation systems. Before the Galvin-driven executive change there, Navteq had been unprofitable. With the right CEO at the helm, Navteq advanced to profitability and shortly after was sold to Nokia for $8.1 billion.

The Board's Role as Guardians of the Venture and the Investors' Money

Recruiting an effective board of directors is as critical as, and sometimes even more important than, selecting key members of the management team. The board is called upon to help provide strategic direction, assist with important external constituencies such as suppliers, bankers, investment bankers, and investors, help ensure effective incentives are in place such as stock options or founder shares, and provide advice and consent on major capital spending and operating issues.

An effective board must receive accurate and timely information in a reporting format that provides the necessary tools to properly direct the business. Management should be certain that the board receives this information several weeks prior to the scheduled board meeting. It's often helpful at board meetings, which may occur from every six weeks to perhaps four times a year, to conduct both a high-level review of the entire business as well as a deep dive into one or two specific areas at least once a year.

The best boards are generally entrepreneurial in their vision while also serving a more measured trustee function for the other stakeholders. They provide a review and check on the actions of management, which, in pursuit of immediate goals, may not remain sufficiently focused on the real end goals. Such management myopia could otherwise result in their failing to put in place the proper management team or operating structure prior to implementation of aggressive growth plans. The board is also entrusted with proper reporting and auditing of results, which is critical particularly for those companies that subsequently choose to become public entities.

Today, in an age of frequent costly hacking attacks, monitoring the security of a company's information and computer systems has become a major board role as well. While guaranteed prevention of hacking may be impossible, the board must assume this role along with management and address as many vulnerabilities as possible. For those companies that either face an immediate security threat or grow so large that the possibility of attempted hacking is very high, the board will often be tasked with forming a cybersecurity committee of the board and being certain that a chief security officer is part of the management team.

Notwithstanding its frequent focus on governance and risk management issues, a key role of many venture capital–backed company boards is to urge the company to accelerate its efforts. The legendary venture capital investor, Arthur Rock (instrumental in the development of Intel and many other companies), was known at board meetings to say repeatedly, "Move faster, move faster."

Board Meetings

Generally the board chair doesn't have too much to do at board meetings other than make sure the agenda is followed, sandwiches are ordered and delivered for lunch, and the meeting ends on time so the VCs can catch their flights. Occasionally, though, board meetings can get highly contentious and almost come to blows and/or threaten the stability of the venture capital investment syndicate.

On one of those occasions, when one of the authors (Len) was chairman of Nanophase Technology, one investor accused another investor (who had helped create the company) of providing misleading information on the status of the company's patents, which the accuser regarded as very important to the company's success. Not surprisingly, the accused took strong offense at this personal attack, and the whole sad show was quickly degenerating into chaos. This meeting was more interesting than most! The chairman's job was to derail the brawl and get the contending fighters to go to their respective corners.

While there may be conflicts over issues at the board meetings, rarely do questions come to an actual board vote. If by chance a question does come to a vote, it generally means that the entrepreneur had not worked to build a consensus on that issue prior to the meeting. A vote can only result in embarrassment for the losing side and heartburn for the entrepreneur.

Some of the better meetings we have attended as board members and investors have included strategic direction discussions, sometimes resulting in complete strategic pivots. When the fate of the company may ride on the outcome, board members are fully engaged, usually with substantive contributions. These discussions can also be quite dangerous, if not fatal, to the survival of the company without considerable industry and competitive domain experience around the table.

Bankers and Suppliers: Sources of Lower Cost Funds

Venture capital is expensive capital. The inherent riskiness of venture capital investment demands the opportunity for comparably lucrative returns. Hence, once the company is further along and more established, it's time to find a banker.

What's needed is a deep banking relationship, not just a one-off lender. High growth requires strong and deep bank lines to see the company through ever growing inventory and receivables expansion. The best bankers thoroughly understand the company, its management, and the industry environment. Rather than panicking and calling the loan if business turns down and difficult, they may work with the company to reschedule payments, and they may also attempt to bring others into the banking syndicate if possible to provide additional credit capacity. They are willing as well to work with the venture capital backers rather than at odds with them.

Major suppliers can also be a source of expansion capital should cash become tight. Relationships with the largest and most important of these suppliers should not be left to the purchasing or operations manager, but instead should receive the time and attention of the entrepreneur.

Following the Money

The venture capitalist doesn't just go away after he has invested in the enterprise. There are, however, varying degrees of involvement depending on the approach and policies of the particular venture capital firm. As a rule, the earlier the stage of the investment (i.e., seed, startup, first-round investment), the more active the venture capitalist will be in following the company and in its decision making. All venture capital investors, whether on the board or not, will want to be informed promptly of all adverse changes as well as major positive developments when this information is available.

Generally the so-called "lead investor" (often the one who sets the initial terms and invests more than the others) will be the most active. Other syndicate members will often look to this lead investor for information and judgment regarding the venture's progress or its lack.

Some venture capital firms have many investments and therefore have a limited amount of time available to spend tracking each investment. Others have fewer investments and tend to focus intensively on each. This can be a function of the particular investment strategy of a given firm. Some choose to take a more diversified approach and make a larger number of investments, playing the odds and striving for aggregated results that represent an acceptable IRR or multiple on their money invested. Others have more of a home run approach, investing in fewer companies and spending more time and effort with each company.

From time to time, the workload of a venture capitalist can change abruptly. This may be due to a problem situation arising for one of his portfolio companies or considerable time required in raising a new investment fund. The time and attention available to follow his other portfolio companies will then diminish.

Finally, some investments just don't require much time. They hit their business plan from the get-go, and so the venture capitalist can spend his time more productively elsewhere. While these bluebirds are welcome, they are also rare.

When Crisis Management Is Required

In the case of seriously distressed situations, the venture capitalist can be expected to take a very active role, particularly if acting as the lead or co-lead investor. In these cases, the VC will become involved in operating decisions and will likely press for management changes, and those with operating skills may even take an active role in the management of the business, however reluctantly.

As previously discussed, when Control Video got into serious trouble, the major venture capital investors engineered the turnaround, kept funding the company week-to-week while the turnaround was in progress, selected a new management team, and then recapitalized the company once it was stable. All this led to the creation of America Online, with its eventual market value of over $350 billion.

A venture capitalist hopefully always adds value, but in some cases can make all the difference.

A major board decision and turning point for the entrepreneur and company is whether the company will remain private or go public and just how it will return a rich reward to its investors. We'll turn our attention to that subject in the next chapter.

CHAPTER 12

The Last Dance: A Successful Exit

The last dance for the venture capitalist and the entrepreneur is a successful exit.

What Constitutes a Successful Exit?

How would we define a successful exit? For an individual venture, at a minimum, to be considered a successful exit, we'd look for one that delivers an annualized return of 20% or better and a minimum three times multiple on the capital invested. For an investor in a fund invested in multiple ventures, we'd consider an overall fund exit with an annualized return of 15% to be successful and one with an annualized return of 20% or greater to be *highly* successful.

Given the inherent riskiness of venture capital investment and the high percentage of ventures that fail, for the investor in an individual venture to consider the outcome as a highly successful exit, we'd set the bar even higher, and call for an annualized return of 30%+. We'd call an annualized return of 40%+ a home run.

Of course, the relationship between the annualized return (its IRR) and the return multiple depends on the amount of time from investment to exit. Some investments achieve a very strong IRR but a relatively low multiple if the exit occurs in fewer years. A larger multiple will likely take more years to materialize. Sometimes a seemingly strong multiple can even represent a modest IRR if the investment goes on for too long. (See Table 12.1.)

For perspective, our team's long-term averages are a return multiple of 3.63, over an average duration from investment to exit of 5.2 years, for an average IRR of 28%.

Table 12.1   Investment Duration and Multiple

Annual IRR	Multiple @ 5 Years	Multiple @ 10 Years
20%	2.5	6.2
30%	3.7	13.8
40%	5.4	28.9

A Range of Exit Options

Until recently, the venture capitalist and entrepreneur generally hoped the venture capital–backed company would one day *go public* in an IPO (initial public offering). In recent years, however, for reasons to be discussed in this chapter, other exit options have emerged more frequently. These options include (1) sale to or merger with generally larger, complementary companies as well as (2) continued private fundraising, where the venture's stock is sold to a small number of private investors and remains private. The latter is sometimes referred to as a *no-exit exit.*

Generally those companies that are merged into or sold to other companies or are sold to other private investors achieve less publicity but can still be very significant. In the past, an IPO or a sale to/merger with another company were about the only real options available for a successful exit. While both of these exit options remain important, they are now joined by the no-exit exit option, which has been implemented recently by some unicorns (a private company valued at $1 billion+) that just keep selling shares privately—both raising new funds and liquidating some of the existing investor holdings—without an end in sight. With this option, the entrepreneur can continue in a control position, take personal money off the table, and hopefully cash out the venture capital investors as well.

Private rather than public exits have become more common in recent years due to the impact of additional regulations for a public company, the flow of capital into venture capital investments from nontraditional major institutional investors, the reduced number of investment banks undertaking IPOs, and a trend for entrepreneurs to want to retain more control over their company for a longer period. This trend has helped create the increasing number of highly valued unicorns.

Realistically, the no-exit exit option is practically available to a limited number of companies. It seems to be most viable for those huge venture capital–backed companies whose private valuations cross the unicorn $1 billion threshold. While the number of unicorns may have increased dramatically the past few years, there still just aren't that many of them. As of late 2016, there were 99 in the United Sates and 176 globally.

This recent exit option developed because major, mostly institutional, investors are willing to invest large amounts at high share prices into these companies in the sometimes overly optimistic hope of an exit at an even higher value, whether being taken out in a private or public sale. Entrepreneurs have come to appreciate this option because, by issuing private stock of different classes with different rights and restrictions, an entrepreneur may be able to retain control of the company while still securing the capital needed for rapid growth, which previously could only be secured usually through a public offering.

The unicorn no-exit exit option has also found favor with some venture capitalists, who no longer find a gaggle of investment bankers ready to take their offspring public at acceptable values. This means that now, more than ever, some venture capitalists feel pressure to swing for the fences with private home run investments and exits.

As we'll discuss later in this chapter, however, exiting a highly valued private company that remains private can be tricky for both the venture capitalist and the entrepreneur, and sometimes the exit needed for a cash return may never occur. Whereas venture capitalists may now often long for one or more of their investments to achieve unicorn status, that can make it more difficult for them to get all their money out while their fund investors may impatiently look for those anticipated rich returns. It can also make it difficult for the entrepreneur and his or her associates to achieve the degree of liquidity they may seek. Be careful what you wish for.

IPO as a Badge of Honor

Going public—an IPO—was once a badge of honor, and for some it still is. It can be potentially a good way to cash out and achieve the longed-for high return. In addition to the cash return, an IPO can be a visible indication of both an entrepreneur's and a venture capitalist's success. For the entrepreneur, it is a tangible sign that his baby has reached the big leagues. For the venture capitalist, it will be noticed by his peers and his investors. A major success will also be noticed by entrepreneurs looking for capital, and most would prefer to have a successful venture capitalist as an investor, so the venture capitalist will secure a stronger deal flow.

Until the public offering, the venture capitalist has been laboring in the company vineyards mostly in anonymity. The entrepreneur may already be highly visible and recognized, or his venture may still be operating in stealth mode under the radar. For both, the IPO may be the brass ring. Everyone likes both the money and the glory.

A public offering can be a good decision for many companies, as they can raise additional capital, often at a higher share price than remaining private. Moreover, if they continue to perform well, they will likely be able to return to the public markets for still more funds to sustain rapid growth.

Remaining Private May Better Meet the Entrepreneur's Needs

While going public may be a badge of honor carrying invaluable bragging rights, a public company represents just the opposite of why most entrepreneurs start their own company in the first place—their drive to achieve without the limitations imposed by public ownership. To be private is to be one's own boss and on one's own, which is where entrepreneurs want to be.

On the other hand, the public companies they'd be running after an IPO are inherently ensnared in regulation and authority. For entrepreneurs who are uncomfortable with what's perceived as the outside interference that exists just with venture capital financing, a public company to them is an excessively regulated world they would rather not inhabit. Those entrepreneurs who are particularly touchy about authority should examine their needs and motivations carefully prior to a decision to go to the public markets, particularly if remaining private—the no-exit exit—is an option.

Remaining private can be a thing of beauty for an entrepreneur. There is less regulation; lawyers and accountants play less of a role, keeping costs lower; directors often are old chums who tend to be loyal and helpful to the founder; contact with stockholders and other stakeholders is more direct rather than through press releases; and just about everyone involved with the company is off the dance floor and out of view, which helps everyone remain calmer and looser. In the private company world, the entrepreneur, always a bit of a buccaneer, may continue to operate on, or a bit over, the edge. Private companies were invented by and for the entrepreneur's satisfaction.

Going Public Can Also Mean Vulnerability to Rumors and Ruin

Running a public company isn't always fun. There are many constituencies that need to be satisfied—government regulators, the legal and accounting advisors trying to keep you out of the regulators' crosshairs, stockholders, and the ever-seeing eye of the financial press, hungry to run the stock up and also to run it down. And these days, the Internet's instant real-time exposure makes it even tougher.

In the old days, a public company management mostly needed to keep feeding brokerage firm stock market analysts good news while soft-pedaling the bad. With the rise of the Internet, exposing every mandated disclosure (and even many that aren't mandated), all news is immediately available and everyone is a stock analyst.

The old adage was, "Buy on the news and sell on the rumor," but now rumor is often the news itself. Even a rumor devoid of factual verification can devastate a public stock and ruin a company almost instantly. Controlling the news has become essentially impossible, and so it has become extraordinarily difficult to manage a public company's stock price. That's one reason why the average tenure of a public company CEO keeps getting shorter and is now down to about four years.

Other Risks of Going Public

Keep in mind that in going public, only a portion of the company may have been sold to the public. The entrepreneur, his close associates, and sometimes the venture capitalists as well maintain sizeable shareholdings whose value they hope to continue to build. The Internet's relentless vigilance and news cycle create huge pressure for a company to report favorable earnings and results, quarter-after-quarter, no matter the impact on the company's long-term health, competitive position, and growth prospects.

Only a limited number of companies, such as Amazon, Alphabet (aka Google), and a few others, which have demonstrated sustained extraordinary growth and growth prospects, are able to convince the market that they don't need to focus so much on near-term earnings.

In addition, a successful public offering can leave the venture capital–backed company vulnerable to the sin of raising too little money for the long term and at too early a stage of development. The public market is like riding a tiger; when the tiger is hungry, you keep throwing him raw meat, and when he is full and doesn't want any more, you need to hold on and keep riding until he is hungry again. It is very difficult to time when the market will be really hungry.

Worse yet, the public offering may not raise as much as was planned. Perhaps when the company hits the offering window and goes public, the underwriters are only able to sell just one-half to two-thirds of the stock that the company needs to sell to maintain a competitive financial structure, or the expected offering price is cut, or both. Perhaps competitors who are also going public have been better positioned, or just luckier with timing, and succeed at raising all the money they require for the foreseeable future and are able to ride out the storm. Raising too little money too soon can be unsettling at best and fatal at worst. And here's still one more risk—on rare occasions, the underwriters announce that the offering is complete, but then several major investors don't show up with the funds, virtually guaranteeing disaster.

Surprisingly, going public could also narrow your market for subsequent capital-raising. Now that the stock is public, investors who are only interested in private companies (and the gain from a potential IPO), such as most venture capitalists, will be unwilling to invest anything further in the company unless the stock is priced as a complete steal. The agreements many venture capital firms have with their investors preclude any investment in public companies. Venture capital investors are interested in private companies, in getting in early and getting out at a high price, not in buying the stocks of public companies, even when they are undercapitalized and desperate to sell more stock at bargain prices.

The few firms that specialize in emerging public companies will normally exact their penalty share price discount for the perceived high risk in the undercapitalized public company. Should the undercapitalized public company fail to achieve the continuing strong support of its principal underwriters, it may be unable to raise any money at any price, even in the public market through a secondary offering. The old adage, "Get all the money you can when you can," often applies not only to venture capital fundraising rounds, but also to public offerings.

Beware of Investment Bankers' Inherent Drive to Go Public

While the initial public offering historically has been the proud product of the venture capital industry, the VC will continue to feel proud only if he pushes for the IPO when the timing is really right from a longer-term perspective. If the venture capitalist encourages his investee companies to go public prematurely, he does a disservice to the public, to his companies, and to the venture capital industry.

Unfortunately, too many investment banking firms will offer to take public almost any company where there is a demand for the company's initial offering shares, even if that really isn't the best choice for everyone at that time. While the investment bankers would prefer that there is a strong first-day bounce (i.e., run-up in share price) so that their favored clients who bought those initial shares can make money on a fast exit, and continuing strong performance of the stock is desired, the main factor for most investment bankers is the fees they can earn on the stock offering. Those fees are the lifeblood of their business. At the risk of offending any of our readers who are investment bankers, some investment bankers would take public a ham sandwich if the demand were sufficient.

When a company decides it is time to exit and cash in on at least a portion of its equity, the major partner in planning and executing the exit is an investment banker. Investment bankers are financial shepherds to the fledgling exiting company. They are experts in advising a company on how to raise capital in the public markets. Some also have extensive networks of money contacts through satisfied clients from earlier deals, and therefore can also arrange a private placement for the company with reasonable fundamentals if it is not ready to go public.

Of course, there are many high-quality investment bankers, too. A quality investment banker, while interested in earning a big fee, will not advise a company to seek a public offering unless he truly believes, based on substantial evidence, that the company is ready to undergo the rigors of a public offering and can survive, if not prosper, in the aftermarket. Unfortunately, however, with their fee orientation, some investment bankers are just not always concerned with whether the company can do well for its investors post-IPO. It's nice if it happens, but investment bankers are not in the nice business.

Investment Bankers and Venture Capitalists Are Not the Same

Investment bankers and venture capitalists can sometimes seem like they are cut from the same cloth. After all, they both make their money off of their hard work from fees, investee company income, or capital gains. There are, however, several distinctions between the two breeds.

An effective investment banker is generally more of a salesperson than the typical venture capitalist, who takes more of a buyer or investor orientation. Remember, the venture capitalist needs to be sold by the entrepreneur seeking funds, and in fact buys a share of the venture on behalf of his investors.

The investment banker, on the other hand, must first sell the successful company on retaining his firm, in competition with many others, as the company's underwriter for its stock sale. Then he must keep the company sold on his services until he can undertake a major transaction, must then sell the company's stock to investors (some savvy, some not), either privately or to the public market, and then must keep selling the company to help maintain or, better yet, grow the price in the aftermarket. Not surprisingly, the investment banker is attuned to the market, and to what kind of company the market will or will not buy, at what price and in what dollar amounts.

The venture capitalist is more concerned with creating real value. Unless real value is created, the venture capitalist may be unable to exit his firm's investment on a positive basis. He may never see a return *of* the money, never mind a return *on* the money.

Interestingly, investment bankers may attempt to raise funds privately from venture capitalists, either in place of or in advance of an IPO, or even following an IPO. However, such deals are quite hard to sell. Experienced venture capitalists tend to be leery of investment banker–offered investments because of their inherent role and inclination differences, as well as due to an aversion to paying the higher share price that needs to incorporate the investment banking fee.

The Groupon Story: A Post-IPO Nightmare

The public offering of the well-known Chicago-based company Groupon is an interesting illustration of the potential perils of succumbing to less than fully informed stock market demand. For anyone not familiar with Groupon, it is a company that distributes "a deal a day" for local merchants—discount coupons on behalf of its clients, typically local businesses such as restaurants, hair- and nail-care places, and other primarily service providers.

Groupon was remarkably fast out of the gates, a veritable race-horse of a venture. Bookings and revenues grew at lightning speed, driving its valuation above $1 billion after just 16 months in business, the fastest company ever to reach this milestone.

Rumors were adrift that Groupon would be acquired by Google for many billions of dollars. According to *Inc.com*, Groupon turned down a $6 billion offer from Google. Following this alleged rejection, the investment banking community, including a number of major firms, decided that there would be strong demand for the company stock at a very high price.

To say they were right would be an understatement. Offered on Nasdaq on November 4, 2011, when it was just three years old, at $20 a share, according to *Bloomberg* representing a valuation of nearly $13 billion, the stock traded that same day as high as $31.14 (trans-lating to a valuation of nearly $20 billion) before closing the day with a 31% gain to $26.11 (translating to a valuation of $17 billion). The *Chicago Tribune* reported that only Google's initial public offering in 2004, which gave the company a valuation of $23.1 billion, ranked higher at that time. According to the *Chicago Tribune* report, Groupon had sold 35 million shares, raising $700 million, in an offering that was seen as a milestone for the company, and also for Chicago, as well as for the Internet-based promotional discounting industry it is credited with inventing. For perspective, Groupon had sold only about 5% of the company, a small portion for an IPO. It was believed by some that offering such a limited share of the company contributed to the remarkably high share price and valuation.

In retrospect, Google appears to have been fortunate in being spurned by Groupon. While Groupon had figured out how to arouse consumer demand with its discount offerings, many clients providing those discounts soon discovered inadequate value for them in those steep discounts and stopped using the company. As a result, Groupon has reported mostly losses quarter-by-quarter, as it has struggled to transform itself by broadening its product offerings. Its stock price has plummeted from that $26.11 close on November 4, 2011, to below $4 as of early 2017.

While the Groupon founders and the investment bankers appear to have done very well indeed, some of the venture capitalists who funded the company's late rounds prior to the IPO didn't do as well, depending on when and for what price they were able to sell. With such a limited initial offering, not all venture capital buyers were able to sell their shares right away. Hence, many of those that bought the Groupon stock other than very early have lost heavily.

About all that can be said for sure is that the venture capitalists, in hindsight, would have preferred to sell the company to Google or another buyer willing to pay for the entire company. And perhaps Google or another buyer would have been able to find a way to turn this company into a source of profits worthy of the price they might have paid. That we will never know.

In fairness to all concerned, it is not known whether Groupon management and the investment bankers recognized the company's fundamental business model problems. If they did, perhaps they feared that Google or another suitor would recognize those problems during due diligence and walk away from the deal, and so they were simply trying to cash in through the public market before too late. On the other hand, notwithstanding the company's $413 million loss in 2010 according to *Inc.com*, it's easy to get caught up in the excitement of rapid revenue growth and the prospects of going public. Look at all the disasters coming out of the 2000 dot-com bubble.

Lessons Reinforced by Groupon's Story

During periods of booming new-issue markets, the go-public pressure can be difficult to resist. When companies go public, venture capitalists, if they can sell their stock (which is often but not always the case), can then report realized gains and distribute real money to their investors, rather than simply reporting book markups. That helps the venture capitalists when they try to raise additional investment funds.

If too many of the VC-backed issues that have not yet been liquidated decline, however, then like most financial excess, this catches up with everyone at some point. Stocks boom and bust, the public eventually gets weary (and wary), and the new-issue process goes through another down cycle, often for a number of years. Noted venture capitalist Arthur Patterson once described those boom-and-bust cycles of venture capital returns (which often depend largely on new public-issue markets) as eight years of plenty and six years of famine.

Timely Liquidation Less Risky than Betting on Volatile Public Markets

The Groupon new-issue experience, while admittedly an extreme, is not unique. IPOs often reflect a degree of irrational exuberance. Over time, about two-thirds of all venture capital–backed new issues decline in value post-IPO and stay below their offering price. This is one of the major reasons that venture capitalists generally seek to sell their now-public stock as soon as possible after an IPO, and it even argues against attempting to take a company public if it can be sold in its entirety for cash.

There Are Exceptions: The Nanophase Technologies Story

Of course, there can be times when going public, even waiting for such an exit long enough for some to feel like it's an eternity, proves to provide a better exit outcome both for investors and entrepreneurs. Another Chicago metro area venture, Nanophase Technologies, one of the first nanotechnology companies, and perhaps the first to go public (in 1997), represents such an exception.

Eight years after its 1989 founding, the venture capital members of its investment syndicate were getting tired and longing for an exit. Happily, sufficient revenue was apparently booked to find several quality investment bank underwriters who agreed to take the company public.

While the IPO was successful as to both price and cash raised for Nanophase, much of the projected revenue did not materialize. Unfortunately, most of the company's customers were in Asia, and when the Asian economic crisis of 1997 (known as the "Asian Flu") hit, shortly after the IPO, many customers canceled their orders. Not surprisingly, the Nanophase stock price crashed. Remember how unforgiving quarterly reporting can be. For the investors, including the venture capitalists, there had not been enough time to sell, so they were caught holding their stock and needing to continue to help build the company.

Anxiety remained high as things were not going all that well in finding additional/replacement revenue. Then, in a fluke of fate, President Clinton mentioned very positively the field of nanotechnology in a major speech, and the company's stock took off like a rocket. The venture capitalists were able to exit at a very high price.

High-technology venture capital investing is not for the faint of heart.

Sale to or Merger with a Complementary Business

For many reasons, a public offering is not always a realistic possibility. The overall stock market may be depressed, so maximum value cannot be realized. Or perhaps stocks in your specific industry group may be temporarily out of favor. Or maybe the company cannot afford the expense of a public offering.

In certain fields, such as biomedical, long-term value may be enhanced by an alliance with a major company, bringing the required deep pockets and broad distribution capability. The sale of the company to or merger with a complementary business can be a successful alternative both for the entrepreneur and the venture capitalist.

When venture capitalists first evaluate an investment, they attempt to judge whether an exit will most likely be by sale or merger, or via an IPO, or in a few cases while remaining private in a no-exit exit. If the company has billion-dollar exit potential within the typical venture capital exit window of five to ten years, then a public offering may be the preferred method of exit. However, when the time comes to exit, it can often be a close judgment call on which method to use, depending on the state of the markets and the financial and operating state of the company.

Benefits of Being Acquired: The Cleversafe Story

The November 2015 exit of Chicago-based data storage and security company Cleversafe to IBM for $1.3 billion is a good illustration of how selling to a corporate acquirer can make sense. The company had grown rapidly over a ten-year period. Major customers were on board, the company was growing at double digits, and it was likely soon to achieve positive cash flow. Needless to say, after ten years, the VCs and their individual investors were more than ready for a cash-out.

A key constraining factor, though, was that the sales cycle is long, and missing several major customers in any quarter could hit cash flow and revenue hard—not a good position for a newly public company whose stock would likely crater in the face of a missed quarter. The IPO markets were also a bit uncertain, with companies going public at high values at that moment, but with signs of a possible market bubble on the horizon.

Investors in Cleversafe included a number of major venture capital firms, including our own Batterson Venture Capital, a co-lead investor in the Series A round. Cumulatively Cleversafe had raised—and spent—$100 million, which actually represented good capital efficiency for a data storage company, which can often require over $200 million in capital prior to an exit. Nevertheless, to continue to build the company to the next level privately would undoubtedly take significant additional capital, further diluting the current shareholders.

Given that situation, the $1.3 billion exit price offered by IBM was clearly a desirable exit option. Many of the shareholders would realize more than ten times their capital invested, and some of the earliest investors would receive a multiple of over 40 times their investment. That's a true home run exit. IBM also represented a good home, with plenty of capital for growth, and was a safe company to be acquired by as to confidence with closing the deal and getting paid. The Cleversafe board voted, as did the majority of investors, to sell to IBM.

In this case, was money left on the table by not going public? Not likely, as the new-issue stock market went into a tailspin shortly after the acquisition. Had an attempt been made to IPO, Cleversafe would likely have been caught in the downdraft as the market fell, and perhaps the IPO attempt might have even been abandoned, with considerable damage to the company.

Issues to Consider Before Selling the Baby

Before the sale of a company like Cleversafe is undertaken, if the entrepreneur is still in control (which was not the case for Cleversafe), he and his board need to consider whether he is emotionally prepared to part with his creation and, if so, whether he is prepared to accept a realistic price. Most entrepreneurs say that they would sell their company; after all, theoretically at least, everything has its price and everything is for sale to the profit-maximizing economic person. However, once the day of sale reckoning approaches, many entrepreneurs may experience seller's remorse and refuse to conclude the sale or merger.

Venture capitalists are often in a formal control position, particularly in a capital-intensive company like Cleversafe. Nevertheless, if the entrepreneur is still the CEO, pushing the entrepreneur too hard can have adverse unintended consequences. Entrepreneurs are often rightly concerned over whether they will continue to play their desired role under new ownership, and whether their employees and other continuing stakeholders will get a fair shake under often-absent ownership.

On the other hand, having a creative entrepreneur still in control as the exit approaches can have its advantages, as the case study we're about to present will illustrate. The former president of a major antivirus software company created CyberSource/Beyond.com over a barbershop in Palo Alto, California, the center of Silicon Valley. The company was formed in 1996, prior to the Internet bubble, to provide downloading of software (Beyond.com) and the transactional software tools that the Internet's early prospectors would need to sell their wares on the Internet (CyberSource.com).

The entrepreneur was still in charge when the time for an exit appeared reasonable, and he decided to split the two product lines of the company into two distinct companies and take both companies public separately. A more traditional MBA-type might not have thought of that strategy and instead taken a more conventional route, keeping the entity as it had been configured.

The entrepreneur's strategic creativity paid off big. Benefiting from two IPOs, early investors received over 41 times their investment in just three and a half years. Sometimes it's best to leave the captain on the bridge all the way through the exit as he may see and capitalize on unconventional exit opportunities that passive investors could never imagine.

In the end, Beyond.com was not successful, but CyberSource was sold to Visa International for several billion dollars a number of years later. For those investors who held on all the way to that sale, there were essentially three exits for one investment—not bad for three guys who started over a barbershop. In this case, the entrepreneur was as concerned with maximizing exit value as he was with holding onto his baby.

Truly "All's Well that Ends Well"

The exit, in whatever form, remains a critical, if not the most critical, element of a successful venture capital investment. Good beginnings and an attractive investment price are important, as are fast and strong developments resulting in high growth, but in the end, it's the exit that matters most.

Interview with a Successful Entrepreneur

In this chapter, Sanford Morganstein, former president and chief executive officer of Dytel Corporation, which started up in Chicago's nearby suburb of Arlington Heights, Illinois, replies to the author's questions concerning the venture capital fundraising experience from the entrepreneur's perspective. (This interview has been reprinted with the permission of Sanford Morganstein.) Mr. Morganstein successfully raised both seed and early-stage venture capital for Dytel, a designer and manufacturer of innovative telecommunications products.

Question: What are the main problems facing the early-stage entrepreneur in the venture funding process?

Mr. Morganstein's Reply: Many venture capital organizations pay more attention to early-stage financing because of the higher potential returns concomitant with the higher risks that are associated with these investments. The problem for the early-stage entrepreneur is the great imbalance between the entrepreneur's vital need to raise money, compared to the venture investor's need (or, more accurately, lack of need) to participate in any single investment. For the early-stage company, getting funded is an absolute "do or die" situation, whereas for the venture investor, there are plenty of companies from which to choose. Perhaps a better way to state this is, if an investor passes on a particular investment, his loss is a loss out in the future, when and if the company is successful. On the other hand, if a company does not get financed, it is most likely disaster for the company. The investor and the company simply do not have the same level of need to close a deal.

Venture Capitalist's Response: Mr. Morganstein correctly perceives the imbalance between most entrepreneurs' critical need for cash, particularly in the early-stage company, and the venture capitalist's need to make this particular investment. However, once a venture capitalist focuses a considerable portion of his most important resource (after money), his time, on an investment, he is reluctant to walk away from the investment opportunity unless a major red flag makes an unwelcome appearance. The best time for the entrepreneur to be raising money is always when he doesn't really need it—this goes for both debt and equity.

Question: How does this imbalance cause problems during the entrepreneur/venture capitalist relationship?

Mr. Morganstein's Reply: For one, the venture capital investor is extremely busy. He or she is researching several proposals, is probably on the boards of portfolio companies, and is called on from time to time to assist in some problem situation. When an entrepreneur sends a business plan to a potential investor, he wants a quick answer. Given that the venture investor is busy and does not share the company's urgency to make the investment, delays inevitably result. A proposal which is not going to go anywhere will probably get a courteous rejection very quickly, but a proposal that gets attention will take a good deal of time (I expect an average is six months). During this time, of course, the entrepreneur is in limbo.

This same imbalance leads to another problem. The entrepreneur must look under every stone to find his or her funding. On the other hand, because venture capitalists are so busy, they don't like to compete with each other. If a company is lucky enough to find two potential investors and is working seriously with one of them, one or both of the potential investors may lose interest. They are simply too busy to waste time on an investment which will not select them.

This imbalance could also lead to problems at the negotiating table. Here's where the importance of a good venture investor comes in. The good investor, one who is interested in building companies and making a good return, will not try to extract a pound of flesh. The experienced investor will realize that exercising too much power will damage the company if the investment goes forward.

Nonetheless, with the present high level of venture money and with a lack of sufficient numbers of experienced investors, many venture capital companies are hiring relatively inexperienced staff people who make it unnecessarily difficult for the company. We have met potential investors who are quite pleased with the imbalance I have described. They perceive that it always works for them. I am not making a comment on the fairness of the process—it doesn't have to be entirely fair—I am only pointing out that the imbalance of the needs of the entrepreneur and the investor is the biggest problem a company has in seeking venture financing.

Venture Capitalist's Response: While venture capitalists do not like to be rushed into making an investment decision, financings can be arranged in weeks or even days if the particular opportunity is both urgent and rich enough and if the entrepreneur is flexible as to the terms of the deal once the price is agreed upon. Most venture capital financings get strung out because, even once a price is agreed upon, the entrepreneur and venture capitalist are really continuing to negotiate the terms of the deal up to the final closing.

Mr. Morganstein is correct in his belief that the experienced venture capital investor is interested in a deal which is fair to all concerned. Unfair deals quickly come unraveled, the parties start squabbling, and little or no good is achieved.

Question: Looking back on the venture funding process, what is your overall opinion of it?

Mr. Morganstein's Reply: The process of raising venture capital is very difficult. It is fraught with risk and anxiety, as I will describe in some of the following answers. But, there is one particular positive point that I would like to make.

Others have pointed out that American business, in general, is short-term oriented. Despite the fact that many businesses require a long-term view, many corporations get nervous in situations which require more than a year or two to reach profitability. In such situations, a short-term, bottom line–driven plan would probably be adopted by the corporation instead of a longer term, albeit more pragmatic, plan.

Venture capital is pretty different. Venture investors know that they are in a situation which will usually require from five to seven years to mature. In this respect, the venture capitalists are more "strategy" oriented, and are more like others, particularly the Japanese, who, on the whole, take a longer-term view of business success.

While I think overall that the venture capital process is extremely difficult for the early-stage company, it is certain that if there were no venture capital process, we at Dytel would not have started the company. While the process is difficult and unbalanced, as I have pointed out, it is certainly one that we entered into with our eyes open. Many times we wished that somehow it could work differently, or that we could put it behind us faster than we in fact did, but overall we learned what it was we had to do.

Anyone who is thinking about immersing himself or herself in this difficult process should be buoyed by the fact that once the investment is made, a long-term partnership will ensue. It provides a real opportunity to create successes which require more time than would otherwise be available. The patience and long view of the venture investors are hard to match anyplace else. It gives the entrepreneurial businessman the time and wherewithal to do his thing.

Venture Capitalist's Response: There are a number of objections which entrepreneurs may raise to venture capital—it is too expensive; why use it if you don't require it—just bootstrap your operation; it takes too long and is too much hassle; too much money in the wrong hands can be worse than too little; and the venture capitalists never really take the time to understand the business and yet intervene in critical decisions.

Entrepreneurs still often want the money, though, because as Mr. Morganstein indicates, money which is well and carefully spent buys time, resources, and at times an insurmountable lead over the competition. This lead is critical to success in those industries and for those products which, while innovative, are not one-of-a-kind.

Occasionally an entrepreneur comes along whom excess cash manages to kill. He can't stand prosperity. Venture capitalists prefer cash conservers.

Most professional venture capitalists will take the time to understand your business. The entrepreneur must understand that in ambiguous, risky situations, honest, even honorable men will differ from time to time.

Question: Why were you successful in raising major venture capital?

Mr. Morganstein's Reply: We were successful, I believe, because we satisfied most of the classic textbook criteria that the venture investor looks for. First of all, we had a good management team. Unlike many technology companies, we recognized early the need for strong marketing skills. We spent a good deal of time recruiting the best marketing executive we could find, and frankly, we were lucky to land him. Our engineering department had a proven track record of managing the development of similar products. Our production operations manager also had done this before.

In fact, the biggest weakness in the management team was almost always perceived to lie with me, since I had never had complete CEO responsibility, despite the fact that I had managed staffs and budgets larger than our entire company will be for several years. A good part of the reason we were successful probably had to do with my ability to overcome this objection. I am probably not alone in overcoming this objection. Many extremely successful ventures were started by people who have had the necessary skills but simply had not done it before. The literature abounds with examples.

We also had a strong, independent board consisting of outsiders. They had previously been involved with fledgling companies, and I believe they provided a good deal of confidence for the investors.

Furthermore, we had a new product which had already demonstrated success in the market. Our customer list was impressive, our product's reliability was excellent, and our market was paying good attention to us. In line with having a proven product, we had, to a certain extent, already begun to prove the company.

We had been in business for two years by the time the investment was closed, and we had proved that we could manage in times of adversity and that we were capable of accomplishing a great deal through a combination of skill and extraordinary effort. At the time we went to raise money, we were a very small company being managed professionally like a big company. Our success was most probably tied to our being able to convince investors of this fact.

Venture Capitalist's Response: The investors backed Mr. Morganstein and his management team despite a lack of CEO experience on Sandy's part because he surrounded himself with a chairman and directors with this vital experience, and because he had previous related leadership experience. In addition, he demonstrated the intuitive ability to make a decision after careful consideration. The team were proven survivors, and had the mark of winners.

Question: Was it more difficult to raise your seed capital or your later-stage financing?

Mr. Morganstein's Reply: I really don't know that my answer to this will be meaningful to others. For us, it was unquestionably easier to raise the seed money, but I think this may have been by chance rather than a result of the nature of raising money. At the seed-capital stage, the stakes were lower, both for the investor and for the company. We were lucky to have raised seed money from those who had strategic interest in participating with us. The early investors were clearly motivated by a desire to create a company in our business area. The profit motive was there as well, but the motivation of the early investors was qualitatively different from the motivation of the venture investors.

Venture Capitalist's Response: Some of the best seed-capital investors are motivated as much by participation in the creative process of business-building as they are by realizing lucrative rates of return on their capital. By and large, the earlier the deal stage, the more risky, so the returns in both capital and psychic income need generally to be higher for the initial investor. Earliest stage investors endure more uncertainty.

Question: How do venture capitalists differ? How are they the same?

Mr. Morganstein's Reply: I have a model of the venture capital community in my mind which, because of its generality, is probably fraught with error. Nevertheless, I look at four kinds of venture investors.

First, there is the inexperienced staffperson who is learning the business. These people can cause problems, and I don't want to say too much more about them.

Then, there are the experienced investors who are usually principals in a venture investing firm. They're interesting because, to a large extent, they themselves are entrepreneurs. These people tend to be very tough on valuation (that is, the percentage of the company they want) and, in my experience at least, have a bias that they know more about the business than the management team does. On the one hand, this can be good since they will be active participants in the business when it goes forward, but on the other hand, if this attitude is exaggerated, the strong-willed entrepreneur will run into conflict with the strong-willed investor.

Next is the experienced investor who works for an investment division of a larger institution. In our experience, these tend to be the most fair, since they don't have the natural tendency to view profits as only going into their pockets or into those of the entrepreneur. They are more likely to look at the prospect of investing in a company as being either wildly successful or savagely unsuccessful. Because of this, they worry less about who gets which percentage—a big part of zero is zero, while a little smaller piece of the moon is fine.

I originally thought that this type of institutional investor would be encumbered by his or her organization. There is a risk of not receiving the high-level management approval needed to make a significant investment. Nonetheless, I suspect that if the lead analyst gives the entrepreneur a reasonable expectation that approvals will be forthcoming, then in all likelihood, the approval will be given even though the process is somewhat slower than that of an entrepreneurial investment firm.

Finally, there is the "seed investor." I include the seed investor in this discussion, although some may feel that a seed investor is not a venture capitalist. A seed investor is usually a private person who invests his or her own funds, although a seed investor can be a strong individual within a large organization which typically does not do venture investing. Usually, of course, the seed investor cannot make the sizable investment really needed to take the company forward, but the seed investor probably does the most to help the company develop.

A seed investor is an early-stage investor who will invest in things that others won't touch. They are as much motivated by the creative urge of sculpting companies as they are by making large returns. The seed investor will give the company an incredible amount of personal time and will guide the growing company in a nondirective, empathetic, constructive style. The amount of time a seed investor spends is significantly out of proportion to the funds he has invested because a good deal of his satisfaction comes from growing companies and executives. Seed investors are one of the best things that can happen to a company.

Venture Capitalist's Response: While   initially   an   institutional investor may be more objective or detached than an investor from an entrepreneurial venture capital partnership, this detachment is difficult to maintain for any venture capital investor after the considerable investment of time, energy, and emotion, as well as money that the normal venture capital investment requires.

Question: Are venture capitalists really interested in company-building or just out for a buck?

Mr. Morganstein's Reply: There are some venture capitalists whom I referred to earlier as seed investors. Their interests probably include people-building, company-building, and money-making. But the tone of the question almost makes it sound like an apology is needed for those who want to make money but don't care about the growth of companies or people. While seed investors do indeed exist, an entrepreneur who expects only seed investors to invest is in for a rude awakening.

Not everybody who is associated with the entrepreneur's company has the same interests in or expectations of the company. This is true of both investors and employees. The entrepreneur who doesn't realize that a good part of his job is to take diverse interests and make something of value from that is probably not prepared to make the compromises needed in the day-to-day management of the company.

We had one venture investor tell us that he doesn't want to make the entrepreneur a friend; he wants to make him rich. Although no one is going to have animus toward another who makes him rich, the point that this investor was making is very well taken. The fuel or lubricant which makes this whole venture capital machine run is money. Seed investors are great, and often essential, but there is no reason to curse a daisy because it's not a rose.

Venture Capitalist's Response: Mr. Morganstein correctly identifies that a company has many constituencies and that the CEO must play to their varied needs and mold those needs so that they all contribute to the success of the company. Part of the CEO's job is to create both confidence and value in and through all the company's supporters.

Question: Are you concerned that venture capitalists will attempt to take over your company later on?

Mr. Morganstein's Reply: No, I'm not concerned about this, and for a variety of reasons. Early in our search for a venture investor, we ran across the companies that, if they didn't want to actually take us over, wanted to have a direct day-to-day impact on the company that bordered on being disconcerting. When we were being interviewed by these investors, we felt like we were being interviewed for a job. We felt like we were going to be hired to implement the investor's plan for building a related group of companies. I don't consider that approach as a "takeover," but with such an investor, I would be extremely concerned about the degree of autonomy I would be able to exercise.

On the other hand, the hands-off investor who lets the company do its thing with gentle guidance will undoubtedly play a bigger role if the business later flounders. In fact, I think many venture investments are structured such that the investor can, indeed, gain a majority control of the board of directors in the event any of several serious problems occurs. I'm not concerned about this eventuality. One reason is that my natural entrepreneurial optimism doesn't let me spend much time on it. Secondly, if things really do get that bad and the venture investors feel that all or part of management can't do anything about it, then management has failed and the company probably should be taken over.

Venture Capitalist's Response: Most venture capitalists would rather not run your company; that's why they invested in the entrepreneur. A number of successful venture capitalists have either run companies before and don't want to now, or have never run a company and don't want to try. The few that do want to run companies are probably not sure what business they want to be in, operating or investing.

Question: Why did you choose the venture capital route to financing your company rather than other alternatives?

Mr. Morganstein's Reply: I don't think we had much choice. We certainly weren't bankable. We may have been able to interest a large company to buy us and merge us into one of their divisions, but no one in our company wanted that. We couldn't have raised more money from our own savings; our seed investors, management, employees, relatives, and friends couldn't provide the kind of money we needed.

There may have been many other sources to look at, but notwithstanding the presence or absence of choice, venture capital was the objective we set for ourselves. We concluded early that venture capital would provide us with the kind of money we needed to position our company through early unprofitable periods. We felt that the venture investor has the necessary long-term view to allow us to sacrifice immediate return for long-term growth. Finally, we felt that the venture investor would leave management with enough equity to keep us motivated to the highest degree.

Venture Capitalist's Response: Some ideas are big ideas and they take big money to implement. Venture capitalists can provide that money, and they can do it early when it's really needed. Time and chance wait for no one.

Question: What traits do you look for in a lead investor?

Mr. Morganstein's Reply: The lead investor has several pretty important roles to play, and these roles may be difficult. Typically, venture investments are made by more than one investor because of the need to share the risk and to make it easier to raise more money should that become necessary. Once the lead investor decides to make an investment, he or she should play an active role in putting the rest of the investment group together.

Just locating potential investors is one part of this assistance, and only one reason why the lead investor role is important. The lead investor has a network of other investors with whom he has probably previously co-invested and with whom he may be on a board of directors. The ease with which an investor can interest other investors says something about how he or she is perceived by his colleagues. If he can't get anyone to go along with him, he may have previously touted some bad investments, or he may have received poor marks in a director's role.

Once other investors become interested in the company, the lead investor's role continues to be important, at least until the time the financing is closed. The reason is that consensus on details of the investment has to be arrived at among the company and the venture investors. If there is more than one venture investor, you end up with the situation of trying to find consensus among a diverse and often terribly opinionated and even stubborn group of people. Reaching such consensus is difficult, and the lead investor should be both strong and influential enough to make sure it happens.

It may be just our experience, but it seems that many early-stage financings get done when the company is in a precarious situation. If the lead investor has decided to make the investment, then it is important for him to ensure that the process of reaching consensus and making all of the finishing touches does not significantly damage the company.

The lead investor can do many things during this period. If the negotiation with the other members of the investment group runs into snags, the lead investor should exercise leadership. If the company needs to pay an important vendor/supplier, or pay a debt, then a bridge loan should be forthcoming (remember—the hypothesis is that the investor has already decided to make the investment). If the company needs an individual to complete or augment the management team, then the lead investor should be using his contacts to help make resumes available.

I think that our company has a particularly strong board of directors who will continue to provide advice and guidance as our company grows. It is important for the lead investor to be someone with solid business experience who will continue to be a major contributor once the venture investment closes. These traits of fairness, integrity, and good sense will eventually be more important than deal-closing leadership.

Venture Capitalist's Response: Pick a lead investor who is not only able, and considered able by his peers, but also willing to work with, and consider the opinion of, other investors, particularly in times of trouble. The lone-wolf investor as a lead can destroy both an investment syndicate and your company.

Question: Did you get a fair deal from the venture capitalists?

Mr. Morganstein's Reply: When the seesaw between investor and company is as unbalanced as I believe it is, it is hard to imagine how it can turn out totally fairly. Maybe it is a tribute to the venture investors with whom we dealt that our situation did turn out in a manner which we consider, on the whole, to be fair.

There are aspects of our situation, on the other hand, which we do consider to have been unfair. We try, though, to take our situation as a whole. We are quite pleased that we have been financed and that we can now get on with the business of running our business.

We feel we received a fair price for the percentage of the company which we sold, and feel it is particularly fair that the venture investors found a way to accept our valuation of our company provided we meet certain objective criteria.

As I stated at the outset, the process doesn't have to be totally fair, but if it is terribly unfair to the point of emasculating management and their incentive, then the investor risks a nonperforming investment. We've had investors tell us that they invest by the golden rule—"He who has the gold makes the rules." So again, the agreements do not have to be totally fair. But, in answer to your question, yes, on the whole our deal was fair.

Question: Was the price of the deal important to you?

Mr. Morganstein's Reply: Yes, but for reasons which may be different from what you would expect. When you look at what the ultimate success of the company will mean to the founders, the price of the deal (meaning, do we give up "X percent" or "Y percent") is pretty immaterial if "X" and "Y" are reasonably close. Even if they are not close, one tends to get lost comparing two very large numbers.

We worked very closely with two potential investors, and "X" and "Y" were in fact very close. What concerned us, on the other hand, was the fact that both "X" and "Y" were close to fifty percent. The fifty percent number meant that, according to the returns we predicted in our business plan, the venture investor would have had compounded returns of seventy percent per year.

This in itself is not a problem; we don't really care about someone else's return as long as ours is fair. But, what the fifty percent figure told us was that the investors viewed us as a very early-stage company and that our achievements up until then—marketing, engineering, and production—were not being given proper consideration. Since the fifty percent figure did not correlate with our notions about desired returns for investors, we could not ascribe the offer to anything but a "venture capital kneejerk." I guess the point of this is that some nonfinancial considerations get mixed into the entrepreneur's perception of a venture capital offer.

In our case, the dilemma was worked out in a creative way. If we performed according to profit target objectives for the first two years of the plan, we would give up "X percent" of the company, and if we did worse, we would give up "Y percent," where "Y" depended on the degree to which we missed the plan. Also, "Y" couldn't be greater than a certain amount.

We were surprised that some investors later expressed opinions that this sliding scale approach to pricing based on profit performance over a period of time is a bad approach, and I never fully accepted their arguments. The nature of such a compromise isn't perfect, of course, since it could push the entrepreneur into making short-term decisions which could affect long-term profitability. There is no doubt that this risk exists, but the very nature of the entrepreneur as well as the venture investor is long-term anyway, and so, in our opinion, the risk was outweighed by the extra motivation we had to perform according to our plan.

Venture Capitalist's Response: Performance formulas are controversial because they can cause the company's management to place their emphasis on objectives which maximize share pricing but minimize or dilute the company's long-term business performance. They can be used if both investors and management are mature and appropriately focused on the long-term success of the business rather than on immediate personal gain.

Question: What was the most difficult part of your experience in raising venture capital?

Mr. Morganstein's Reply: Since we were pretty far along with two different investment firms, the hardest part was to keep them both interested until we received a firm commitment from one of them. As I mentioned earlier, venture investors are among the busiest people around. Given the large volume of proposals they receive, and our assumption that they have a predilection to turning proposals down, we felt that if either of them decided not to compete with the other, then we would lose a potential investor. My earlier point was that it was of vital importance to us to get funded and of somewhat lesser importance for any given investor to invest in us.

We were, therefore, faced with spending a good deal of time with both investment firms. We helped both of them with their investigation and due diligence and doing whatever we could to keep them both interested despite their predisposition against competing with each other.

There were other problems, too. We, of course, had to continue to run our business while we spent a good deal of time with the investors. We had also planned to make some important hires, and we didn't know if we could afford to.

We did find, however, much to our surprise, that our customers were not overly concerned that investors would call them (as part of the investor's due diligence investigation). Customers did mind when they were called frequently by different investors, but this was more of an annoyance factor, and it didn't seem to raise concerns in the minds of our customers about the company's financial stability.

I think that the rest of the process of raising venture capital, while difficult, is not too different from that which is needed to run the business properly anyway. An investor needs a business plan—so does the company. A company needs a management team—investors need to see it. A company needs satisfied customers, and the investors need to see this as well.

Since investors check out customer references, the company must make sure that its customers are being properly treated. Again, a good company must do this whether or not it is raising venture capital.

Venture Capitalist's Response: Venture capital is a very time-intensive business, and in recent years it has become even more so as there have been both more capital and a larger number of high potential deals than in the past. The active venture capitalist is trying to catch the best deals, while also helping revive one or more troubled deals, perhaps raise new capital for his fund (if a private partnership), hire and train new employees, and participate in an industry with its numerous meetings and associations. He has a very full plate.

The entrepreneur must both respect and obtain his fair share of this time if he is to successfully raise capital. Since the entrepreneur cannot be certain of financing until the terms are agreed on and the deal closed, it is best for a time to continue to work with several potential investors. Once a lead investor commits, however, it is time to stop courting others' favor.

Question: How could the venture capital community improve their approach in order to facilitate the money-raising process?

Mr. Morganstein's Reply: I am heartened by this question. It goes back to my answer to the earlier question concerning the obstacles a going company faces in raising venture capital. The fact that the question is asked points out that the venture capitalists realize that all may not be rosy.

First of all, let me point out that the venture capitalists do provide an extremely professional approach. If they're not interested, they let you know very quickly, so that you can begin to knock on some other doors. Also, despite the fact that they are very busy, they are very good at focusing on the prospective investee company so that when you are working with them, they quickly grasp what your business is about. Further, they have been involved with many companies at similar stages of development, and so they can easily point out deficiencies in the company's planned cash flow, inventory, distribution, and so on. This experience factor is extremely important. Hopefully, venture capitalists will be careful how they use the "apprentices" who are learning the venture capital business.

The venture capitalists also do a good job of informing prospective companies about what the process is like. Several organizations exist which put on seminars about raising venture capital, and venture capitalists are almost always willing to participate. This book is another example of a service which hopefully will help the entrepreneur learn what he or she can expect when trying to raise venture capital. Of course, once an investment is made, the venture capitalist is in an extremely good position to facilitate the company-building process. They usually will be members or observers of the company's board of directors. At this stage, they bring their experience and business skills to bear on the strategic decisions facing the young company. Furthermore, they are in a position to help the company with business contacts that the company might not otherwise have. Some refer to this as "know-*who*," versus know-*how*.

Venture Capitalist's Response: A professional venture capitalist, like the entrepreneur he backs, mostly learns his business through the world of hard knocks. The industry does need to work on methods to help develop new members of the community other than through baptism by fire.

Question: What criteria did the various venture capitalists use to evaluate your deal?

Mr. Morganstein's Reply: All of the venture capitalists we talked to considered the strength of the management team to be extremely important. It's probably a cliché to point out that an investor would rather invest in a company with excellent management with an okay product than the other way around. Others, however, feel that if the product is extraordinary but management is only so-so, they can strengthen the management team after the investment is closed. In any case, one of the important characteristics of the management team is its record of success in a situation closely related to the situation in the new company.

The investors certainly are interested as well in companies that are doing something new and different. They will be more favorably disposed toward a company whose product or service presents a strong economic incentive for the customer to purchase the product or service.

We would like to believe that one of the criteria used to evaluate the pricing of the deal is the rate of return the investment would provide. As I pointed out earlier, I don't think this was done in our case, and it's very difficult for this to be done in the case of any early-stage company because of the extremely high degree of uncertainty inherent in the young company's own projections.

I think the venture capitalist also looks for a company which is in a business area of overall interest to the investor, such as computers, medical equipment, software, and so on. Some have mentioned that they look particularly for new market niches, and I'm sure that this criterion was used in our case.

Also, I think the venture capitalist uses geography as one criterion in making an investment decision. If the prospective company is close to the investor, the company has a better chance—other factors being equal—since the investor would welcome the opportunity to reduce his travel.

Question: Is venture capital money expensive money?

Mr. Morganstein's Reply: At first glance, venture capital money is very expensive. An investor is looking for forty to fifty percent compounded return on his investment. If a company borrowed $1.00 from a bank and paid fifteen percent interest per year, at the end of five years the company would pay back $2.01 in combined interest and principal repayment. At forty percent, this same dollar would cost $5.38.

So, it appears that venture money is expensive, but there's another way to look at it. Most companies that are venture-funded are not candidates for bank financing, at least not for the same amount of money which could be made available by a venture investor.

Maybe this sounds like an apology for the high rate of return a venture investor gets, but I don't think my example is too far-fetched. In many cases, a company could not borrow as much as ten percent of the amount a venture investor would invest. Over-all, you may have to conclude that venture money is expensive, but you get a lot for the price.

Venture Capitalist's Reply: An experienced venture capitalist can rate the riskiness of your deal on a one-to-ten scale. Take some of the risk out of the deal for him, and he may give you a better price.

Question: What techniques did you use to sell your deal?

Mr. Morganstein's Reply: I believe that a good venture capitalist is motivated by the desire to build companies as well as the desire to make big returns. In our company, all of the key management were very enthusiastic about our business, our potential, and what we had already accomplished. We made sure we communicated our enthusiasm to each potential investor, and hoped it was infectious.

But, overall, I think that techniques used to sell the company to an investor are similar to those used to run the company. We tried very hard to get trade press coverage of our new product. The cov-erage was impressive and very positive, and we used reprints with potential investors and continue to use them for potential cus-tomers. We started early to present ourselves as a company with a strong commitment to customer service. Our customers and investors both liked this. The investors were favorably impressed with us because they spoke to customers who had had the benefit of our customer service. We were in business for two years before we raised venture capital, and were able to point out to poten-tial investors that we could manage our business and plan and perform according to plan.

There were a couple of things we did which fall outside this premise which were specifically related to attracting venture capital. One of these tactics was chosen particularly to raise our proposal to a higher degree of attention than it would have otherwise received from the busy venture capitalists. I became personally involved in a nonprofit organization which supported other entrepreneurial companies. I got to meet several venture capitalists through this organization, and I believe that when the time came to present our business plan, it was somewhat easier for me.

Venture Capitalist's Response: Once the money is raised, the real work of company-building begins. An entrepreneur who can sell a venture capitalist should have sufficient skills to sell his product. However, neither venture capitalist nor entrepreneur should ever forget that the product marketplace is often less forgiving than the venture capital deal marketplace. Some entrepreneurs are better at selling their vision than at closing product sales.

Question: Several venture capitalists turned you down. What did you learn from these rejections?

Mr. Morganstein's Reply: Grace.

Some of the reasons for the rejections we had in fact anticipated as problems and risks associated with our new business. When it came to rejections because of problems we knew about, we felt disappointment, but didn't learn very much from it. These rejections did, however, remind us that we should perhaps focus more on these problems and try even harder to address them. They could have just as easily turned us down out of concern that our market wouldn't develop.

Some of the rejections, however, made little sense to us. My favorite is the "fear of competition" rejection. We have a unique product and, if it is any good, there would certainly be competition. The opposite pole of this kind of rejection is the one which in fact fully recognizes the uniqueness of the product. This produces fear of there being no market for the product.

We felt that the people who turned us down because of "fear of competition" fall into the category of those who are looking for reasons not to invest. Maybe my view of this comes out of hubris, but overall I don't think we learned valuable lessons from these rejections. A venture capitalist who turns a particular investment down feels that the problem he or she sees can't be fixed. Otherwise, he would invest and then participate in fixing the problem. Maybe we would have felt differently if someone had told us that they would invest "if _____."

Actually, we did get one such rejection from someone who didn't like our initial valuation of the company. He said that he would consider the proposal if the price were different. By the time we received the rejection, we had in fact already modified our initial valuation and were too far along with our ultimate investor to go back and start a price negotiation with the new one.

Question: Would you do it again?

Mr. Morganstein's Reply: Not soon.

PART

IV

Looking Ahead: What's to Come

CHAPTER 14

The Foreseeable Future

While this book was written to help both the investor and the entrepreneur learn what they need to know to succeed today, venture capital is all about the future. Hence, to succeed in venture capital today, you need to think right now about the future. Of course, we hope as well that this book remains helpful for you for many years to come.

We're bullish on the future of venture capital. For anyone who thinks the greatest innovations are behind us and questions how much is still left to invent, we would argue that the greatest days of innovation and hence of venture capital opportunity are still to come. While we doubt the readers of this book are such skeptics (if you were, we doubt you would have picked up this book), if you are, we offer a grateful thanks for leaving the wealth opportunity from future innovations in the hands of those of us who can still dream and think big.

The Case for Even Greater Innovation and Venture Capital Opportunity

From a natural historical and anthropological perspective, human beings as a species are just now undergoing the growing pains of early adolescence. In a world that is billions of years old, the modern human species as we know it has been around for only about 200,000 years. Civilization as we know it is only about 6,000 years old. Like adolescents, we are still developing the tools, concepts, understanding, and judgment which will serve us well as we come to a fuller realization and exercise of our powers. But we don't think you acquired this book to explore natural history and anthropology, so let's get real.

The tools and technologies that are rapidly emerging will be much more powerful and useful than much of what we've seen to date. Think about computers and information technology as an example. When the authors were in college, a computer filled a large room, generated so much heat that it required costly air conditioning, and yet had far less power than today's typical smartphone we all carry around. Back in our business school days, a simple calculator whose only functions were to add, subtract, multiply, and divide cost more than a day's pay for a typical young executive.

Moore's Law has changed all of that, enabling the modern digital revolution. In 1965, Gordon Moore, the co-founder of Intel, observed that the number of transistors per square inch on integrated circuits had doubled roughly every year since their invention. Based on that observation, he essentially predicted that computing would double in power roughly every one to two years as well. That prediction, of course, was prescient and anticipated the massive increases in computing power that we all enjoy today.

Similarly, we have seen awesome advances in medical and biotechnological capabilities over the past 10, 20, 30 years. The mysteries of our genomics have been solved, and a result has been the ability to tailor lifesaving drugs to specific genetic problems. A sister-in-law of one of the authors has been able to survive and live a normal life for many years despite chronic leukemia that would have killed her 20 or 30 years ago due to a drug that addresses her specific genetic issue.

We could go on and on, but the point should be clear—we are already enjoying the benefits of technological advances we could not have imagined 50 years ago. Foreseeing enhancements to present known and working technologies and their future combination and integration into more complex forms provides a window on the opportunity for even greater technological innovations in the years to come.

Importantly, the advances already upon us and behind us represent a technological infrastructure enabling and facilitating future advances. Further advances, as they accrue, will enrich that technological infrastructure even further, enabling advances at a logarithmic pace in many fields. Moreover, entrepreneurs in most fields of technology will be helped further by advances in information technology—software and Internet technology—already behind us. Those advances in information technology will enable knowledge to be built and disseminated more effectively and efficiently than ever before, bringing down the costs of initial startup requirements and shrinking their development timelines.

On top of all that, humans' ever-increasing expectations and aspirations and continued economic development of today's emerging and less-developed parts of the world, along with needs resulting from natural resource constraints, climate change, and other environmental concerns, hold promise for even more innovation than we've seen to date. In addition, demographic, social, and psychological elements are in place that should foster greater entrepreneurial efforts, driving accelerated innovation and its greater utilization, and creating opportunities for increased wealth and human satisfaction and fulfillment.

As discussed earlier, there are now roughly ten million American households with the affluence recognized by the SEC as sufficient to allow investment in venture capital without the strict dollar limitations placed on most Americans. Innovation in the venture capital industry itself—the emergence of online venture capital investment portals with much lower investment commitment requirements than traditional firms—will lower investment barriers, enabling more individuals to invest in this asset class.

Ironically, more traditional venture capital firms like ours, which only allow investments from accredited investors and, even though accessible online, set high minimum investment requirements (our new firm VCapital has a minimum individual investment requirement of $25,000), welcome these new firms. For us, the ability of a venture to attract a large number of other firms' smaller investors represents valuable market intelligence, demonstrating early concept appeal. It's somewhat like virtual market research. If the venture goes on to show progress and has greater subsequent funding needs for expansion, we may be more likely to invest. We may not get in quite as early as before, but the risk when we do get in (which will still be early in the venture's development) will be a bit less, too—an acceptable tradeoff.

Socially, entrepreneurial pursuit of innovation-driven wealth is replacing fields like consulting and investment banking as a chosen avenue for many of our best and brightest. As entrepreneur and professor Steve Blank wrote recently about Stanford (which, despite both authors' Harvard Business School MBA degrees, we recognize as one of the very top universities in America) in the venture capital industry journal, *CB Insights*, "Stanford is an incubator with dorms." He identified 145 different entrepreneurship classes at the university, not just in Stanford's Business School, across 8 departments, including 7 classes at the School of Medicine.

Technology Advancement—and Investment—Opportunities

What does all this mean? What sorts of advancements can we expect and plan for? Here are some we're betting on, in alphabetical order because we can't possibly yet rank these in order of potential:

Advanced materials

Artificial intelligence

Big data and predictive analytics

Biological computers

Biomedical

The conquest of aging

The genome

Immunology

The Internet of Things and of Everything

Nanotechnology

Robotics

Virtual reality

We expect that most these areas will, over the next 30 years, usher in unimagined and unimaginable wonders. Many of these developments will occur within our lifetime. Simple extensions of current scientific and technology trends, merely continuing on established paths without a major shift in perspective as to how the world works and what works in the world, will result in a visible difference in our world. And we can expect even more.

Venture capitalists look out to the foreseeable future, five to ten years ahead, for cutting-edge investment opportunities. While many of these right now can be but dimly perceived, a venture capitalist must be farsighted. While most major technology developments over the next 30 years have not yet been imagined, those emerging over the next 10 years are beginning now. We won't dig into all these areas here, but let's look at just some of the areas where we believe major venture capital investment opportunities are likely over the next 10 years.

Artificial Intelligence: Computers Becoming Even More Integral to Our Lives

One of the most important of the technology evolutions counted on is something we can hold right in our hand—a computer—and that mini-version, the smartphone. Over the past 60 years, computer processing power has increased over one trillion times. Our computers are storing and processing more complex and greater quantities of data for less money at faster and faster processing speeds. Experts say that the smartphones we all carry around have more processing power than the computer that guided our nation's first manned launch to the moon.

Computers are now listening to us, talking with us, and assisting us in making our lives more pleasant and in making more informed decisions. They have become personal assistants and even extensions of us, and soon will seem more and more like ourselves with a form of consciousness unique to their state. Soon they may pass the test where, for someone who doesn't know that a computer is "speaking," one may not be able to distinguish a computer from a human being.

While the human brain doesn't work in many ways like a computer, despite the frequent comparisons, a computer with brain-like function is likely on the horizon. Computers will seem to think in the way and of the things we do, and will likely also soon outthink us. Once they outthink us, we are in a brave new world, untethered from the past and uncertain of the future.

Christopher Evans, in his illuminating book, *The Micro Millennium* (published in 1979 by The Viking Press), defines intelligence as "the ability of a system to adjust appropriately to a changing world, and the more capable of adjusting—the more versatile its adjusting power—the more intelligent it is." He then goes on to argue that there are six factors that permit an entity to be more versatile in its adjusting power and hence more intelligent. These factors are:

1. Sensation, or the ability to capture data
2. Data storage, or how much information can be stored, how fast, and for how long
3. Processing speed, or how fast the information can be handled and moved into use

4. Software modification speed, or the speed and ease with which the entity can alter its programming and/or produce new programming when conditions require (as well as the ability to make its own modifications)
5. Software efficiency, meaning that little of the processing power is used running the program and that it is error-free, or nearly so
6. The range of tasks that the software permits the entity to perform

Using this definition of intelligence, Evans then sets up a scale to rate various entities on intelligence. This scale is useful in demonstrating the difference that currently exists between human intelligence and computer intelligence and understanding how fast the intelligence gap is closing.

When Evans first wrote his book in 1979, if humans were at one million on his current scale, computers would have been at about 1,000—essentially beating humans in only one category, processing speed. So on his scale, humans in 1979 were considered 1,000 times more intelligent than computers.

This vast difference in 1979 really shouldn't give humans cause for much comfort, though, as Evans noted that it took humans 200,000 years to reach that level of intelligence, whereas the computer had existed at that time for a little more than 25 years, not much time to evolve. Since 1979, or over less than 40 additional years, the computer has made huge strides (including that one trillion–multiple improvement in processing power) toward human-like intelligence, not only narrowing the gap tremendously, but also rapidly accelerating the rate of its narrowing.

The emerging field of artificial intelligence, or putting a computer chip in a device or material that makes it more highly functioning or "intelligent," is currently a darling of venture capital investing. Chips and related electronic devices are now so small (nanotechnology) and cost effective that essentially anything can be made more intelligent, from a car (now a computer on wheels) to a toaster. More intelligence results in new products and new applications of existing products and is producing a Cambrian explosion of new startup companies and venture capital investment opportunities.

Evans also argued that human evolution required humans to develop, possess, and run their own huge "software" packages—to reproduce, eat, see, hear, maintain bodily systems, and so on. A computer does not have these requirements and so its users can concentrate efforts only on the software required for intelligence. This should lop many years off of the computer's evolutionary timescale.

As computer hardware and software develop, including the soon-to-be quantum computer (vastly faster processing in all states simultaneously), the machine itself will be able to help improve its own software and hardware through artificial intelligence, and also design and build its "offspring" through 3D printing and manufacturing. The accelerating rate of computer evolution makes it likely that by 2075 ultra-intelligent machines will virtually coexist with humans.

Will the Computer Be Wise?

What is not clear is whether an ultra-intelligent computer will be wise. Wisdom, as defined by Evans, comes from (1) applying intelligence (2) to seek out and understand information (facts), (3) resulting in knowledge (familiarity, understanding, perception of facts or situations), and (4) then using that knowledge, combined with common sense, to undertake actions or decisions that contribute in a positive way to the development of a person and the wider world.

It would seem that an ultra-intelligent computer could and should be wise, as through its intelligence it will have superior knowledge. The unanswered concern to humanity, however, is whether it will adopt human values and make a positive contribution, or whether it might evolve to create its own values that while perhaps enhancing its own interests might enslave or destroy humanity. In human history, superior knowledge has not always been used wisely to promote positive human values, but instead has at times resulted in destructive impulses. It does seem, however, that the more knowledge a "species" possesses, at least over the period of the evolution of humans, the wiser the "species" generally becomes, so there is hope and precedent for the ultra-intelligent computer becoming ultra-wise.

Notwithstanding such profound questions, what does seem almost certain is that, for the venture capital investor over the next ten years, the computer and its related software and other add-ons will continue to generate a fountain of money.

Big Data and Predictive Analytics: The *Why* of Everything

As computers and other devices become more intelligent, they gather more and more information that is of commercial use, resulting in the further accumulation of big data. *Big data* is just (1) a lot more information than we could assemble and access before there was big data storage and (2) faster processing of the data.

Recently our venture capital team exited, following an investment almost ten years ago that delivered a unicorn-like gain, a Chicago-based company—Cleversafe—that has disrupted the cost, access speed, and security of big data. Lower-cost storage and fast access mean that a great deal of information can now be analyzed—big data analytics—and mined for gems of commercial importance.

Another Chicago-based venture our team is currently backing, a startup called simMachines, has developed software algorithms that can analyze those big data sets in order to predict why there is a certain outcome. If you know the *why* of a particular outcome, it is then possible to intervene in a positive way earlier in a process, for example, with a customer, in order to shape desired outcomes more often.

Biology as a Computer

Just as we regard that machine that sits on our desk as a computer, so we can regard biology as a computer, with DNA as the programming software of human beings. The human genome, the complete set of genes housed in 23 pairs of chromosomes, is both the autobiography and the future of our species.

As our understanding of the ordering and function of the genetic code that constitutes the genome continues, research will focus on directing, controlling, and increasing the power of our human biological computing systems. This will enable numerous advances to continue to occur in medicine. These could include the conquest of cancer, maybe the conquest of aging, and perhaps even a redefinition of death as we experience it.

The farthest reaches of science today are demonstrating that we can apply the rules, codes, and patterns that govern human nature and human life to inanimate matter such as silicon and other advanced materials that make up a computer chip. Fascinating efforts are underway to create biological computers that use the molecules present in nature to store as well as transmit information. These bio-computers, if based on carbon rather than on silicon, would be composed of the most dominant element essential to human life. Depending on the evolution and complexity of their architecture and the sophistication of their programming, these bio-computers could begin their evolution toward brain-like functions and ability. While it may take 30 years or more to reach the vision of a biological computer, it is likely that much sooner—maybe even within the next 10 years or so—many venture capital investment opportunities will emerge, as momentum toward the biological computer accelerates.

Nanotechnology: The Domain of the Very Small

The understanding and application of nanotechnology—the very small—continues at a rapid pace. Nanotechnology was first developed commercially by a couple of startup venture capital–backed companies in the early 1990s. One of these companies was Nanophase Technologies, based in a nearby Chicago suburb, which one of our earlier funds, Batterson Johnson Wang, was fortunate to invest in, capitalizing on our Chicago location and resulting professional network.

Nanophase Technologies was founded in 1989, based on technology developed at Argonne National Laboratory and brought to the venture capital community by Arch Development Corporation (Argonne National Laboratory/University of Chicago Development Corporation).

As a venture capital firm, we were early investors in this field, but as we argue, it is often better (and more profitable) to be early rather than late. Nanophase went public in 1997, but with most of its venture capital investors continuing to hold their shares. The IPO was then followed by a highly successful exit for most of its venture capital investors several years later. Our Batterson Johnson Wang $1.28 million investment resulted in over $18 million on its exit, for an annualized average return of 49.7%.

Nanotechnology is just now, 20 years after the Nanophase Technologies IPO, beginning to revolutionize materials, medicine, robotics, and about any other field it touches. It's been a long haul since the founding of Nanophase Technologies to scale up grams of nanomaterials (particles smaller than a virus) for valuable utilization in products and processes.

The understanding and use of the ultra-small is creating new materials with new properties and new applications, creating major new investment opportunities. This trend will continue well into this century. As in the past, with the discovery and application of such new materials as coal, oil, and cement, nanotechnology—the ultra-small—will enable fundamental changes and new fortunes will be made.

The era of the ultra-small is really just now beginning. Investors, get in early!

Robotics: Machines Come to Life

The further development and combination in robotics of machine learning, artificial intelligence, advanced vision systems, predictive analytics (joined with big data), and virtual reality will open another door for major venture capital gains, we believe in the relatively near term. Robotics is the branch of mechanical engineering, electrical engineering, and computer science that deals with the design, construction, and application of robots and the associated computer systems that control and direct their operations.

A brave new world of highly functioning robots is predicted in the near future to eliminate the need for much of today's hard human labor, freeing humans from exhausting drudgery as well as resulting in a world of material superabundance. All this could reduce major causes of poverty and even war. Micro-robots constructed of nanomaterials might soon be injected into the human body for surgical and other medical purposes. Robots may eventually construct and operate the factories of the future with minimal human touch.

The current decade, to 2020, and the next one, to 2030, will open numerous opportunities for tremendous venture capital gains in robotics. This is because, for the first time, the necessary elements of truly advanced robotics technology are converging. For example, advanced robotics requires advanced vision systems, as it is nearly impossible to do work without manipulating the tools of the work, and this is not possible without the ability to see. Machine vision startups are now applying advanced materials and methods, along with knowledge about how humans see, to create artificial vision systems for robots. These systems, while currently crude, have the near-term potential, as more is understood about the meaning of how to "see," to provide inanimate hardware-enabling robotic consciousness—the accurate perception of the physical environment and the ability to navigate that environment.

Human vision as we know it requires immense processing power and memory recall as well as the ability to make an accurate guess about what is perceived when the image is ambiguous. Accurate machine vision systems will require all of this and more, including the capacity to learn from experience. Several new technologies will assist robots and machines to see and thus to learn from their environment.

Virtual Reality: The Unreal Simulating the Real

A close cousin of big data, predictive analytics, and machine vision is virtual reality. Venture capitalists have helped create and fund so many recent virtual reality companies that investors are beginning to question the venture capitalists' own grip on reality.

According to Wikipedia,

> Virtual Reality (VR) typically refers to computer technologies that use software to generate realistic images, sounds and other sensations that replicate a real environment (or create an imaginary setting), and simulate a user's physical presence in this environment.

You are there in three dimensions!

Early uses for VR include video gaming, medical, and military applications. It has also been used in both product and manufacturing engineering for the automotive, aerospace, and ground transportation industries.

Media presentations, including motion pictures, concerts, and sports viewing, and many forms of marketing are now being transformed by VR. Robotic engineers will soon be able to use VR to simulate for a robot a virtual world that the robot will see as its real world. The robot will then apply lessons learned in its virtual world to the real world, accelerating robot development and deployment.

The challenge for a venture capital investor with these new computer platform–transforming technologies will be to forget the past, as the past will only be prologue and even the present will recede ever rapidly into memory.

The Internet and the Coming "Third Wave"

Driving much of the accelerating technical progress across many of the high-potential areas is the Internet. Steve Case, in his illuminating new book, *The Third Wave* (published in 2016 by Simon & Schuster), views the history and evolution of the Internet in three distinct waves.

1. The first wave was characterized by companies like AOL, Compuserve, and Prodigy, the online companies previous to the full-bodied Internet that drew initial users to the online experience.
2. The second wave brought the transactional and social media companies such as Amazon, Facebook, Google, and Twitter, which engaged the customer and the customer's daily life in the online digital world.
3. The third wave is the emerging present and future of the Internet, in Case's view, where the Internet experience not only becomes the Internet of Things but the Internet of Everything. The Internet of Things is the Internet embedded in all devices, materials, and processes, facilitating communication and information exchange and increasing the intelligence and usefulness of all things. The Internet of Everything is the Internet penetrating all of business, government, and society, with the worldwide web becoming more than the shadow world, but essentially a companion world.

The third wave of the Internet will require coordination, cooperation, and convergence, all good opportunities for entrepreneurs who understand this perspective as well as having technical skills and disruptive ideas. For the venture capital investor, look for the Internet everywhere, as it will likely be not only outside us, but also inside. For the Internet inside of us, medicine is where it will reside.

Biomedical Advances through Information Flow

The rapid advance of medicine in this century has been not only about individual and collective discovery, but also about the communication and dissemination of those discoveries. Historically, some medical developments such as penicillin and other powerful antibiotics were the result of preparation and chance. Some breakthroughs came to scientists in their dreams while some were the product of a long process of trial and error, deduction and induction, theory and experiment. Advances in medicine really began to accelerate when information and discoveries began to be communicated more broadly, through books, journals, then peer-reviewed journals, and more recently the Internet.

The Internet, since it is open to all comers, can both host and disseminate at blazing speed in real time the most recent discoveries and information. It is also essentially free, so accessing the latest information entails little to no cost.

Models for the Cure of Cancer

Progress in cancer research and treatment, as well as the funding of this research (now often through venture capital investment), is a good example of the power of the Internet to advance medicine. As Siddhartha Mukherjee exposits in his book on cancer, *The Emperor of all Maladies* (published in 2010 by Simon & Schuster), over several thousand years there have been many models hypothesized to understand and guide the treatment of cancer. Models can provide signposts that tell researchers and clinicians where to look and what to try. They can be useful, even if mistaken, because at least they can be disproved and new models constructed and acted upon.

Historically, incorrect models have been disproved and new models hypothesized slowly due to the slow spread of information dissemination. While individual attempts at treatment may have proved ineffective quickly, there was no effective way to spread this learning quickly.

While there were books reporting these developments by the 17th and 18th centuries, there were not many timely, widely read, and reasonably comprehensive journals on the subject until 1823, so progress in the development of new cancer models remained slow even into the 20th century. The first medical journal to appear weekly was *The Lancet*, which came out in the UK in 1823. However, at that time, it consisted largely of personal writings; the practice of editorial peer-reviewed journals did not begin until sometime after World War II.

Once peer review came into its own, modern medicine took a giant step forward, and validated information became available to both the medical community and investors. In cancer modeling and treatment, this new openness and validation of data led to a number of new models for understanding and treatment of cancer. Nevertheless, even with this widely available information, the world was lacking sufficient big data to analyze and synthesize into predictive analytics that might enable a definitive model.

Then came an early, powerful foray into big data in medicine—the model for DNA constructed by Watson and Crick in 1953—and nothing has been the same since. It gradually became clear that each individual's cancer is somewhat unique to the individual, and so a model was needed to guide treatments that would eradicate each individual's unique cancer. While trying to trace each individual's unique cancer pathway worked on a very limited basis with a few cancers, the possible number of pathways and genes that would need to be eradicated, altered, or perhaps replaced is so large that even our fastest supercomputers cannot currently model the pathways.

Recently, the new model to eliminate a personal cancer has been to mobilize each individual's unique immune system in order to recognize and destroy the individual's unique cancer. Drugs have been developed to either boost the immune system's ability to kill cancer cells and/or release "brakes" that slow the cancer and enhance the ability of the immune system to fight the cancer. Known as PD-1 inhibitors, these drugs have resulted in several multibillion-dollar anti-cancer franchises, including Merck's Keytruda, used to treat melanoma.

Venture Capital Targets Cancer

These autoimmune drug developments also have stimulated venture capitalists to make investments in various methods to activate the immune system against cancer and in other approaches to treating cancer. The creation and development of the Internet have provided the essential access to the information necessary to quickly and effectively accomplish a deep dive into better understanding cancer and cancer treatments. This in turn has opened the floodgates to investment in cancer-killing drugs and other promising alternative approaches.

VCapital, the authors' recently launched online venture capital investment firm, recently invested in one such approach to the activation of the immune system, combining an *enhancer* compound with existing FDA-approved chemotherapy drugs in a powerful cocktail that is injected directly into the tumor. This new technical approach, employing the chemical enhancer and injecting the cocktail directly into the tumor, permits considerably more chemo to actually penetrate the cancer tumors, killing the cancer cells while also creating a strong immune reaction. In mice with human colon cancer, this approach has cured a high percentage of the mice. Moreover, due to the cocktail's direct injection into the tumor, less chemo is required than with traditional methods, even though more actually penetrates the cancer tumors. This results in less anticipated side-effects while killing the metastasis and making the mice immune to the recurrence of the cancer.

This venture, called Intensity Therapeutics, was authorized by the FDA to begin human trials in early 2017. Needless to say, should this approach work in humans as it has in mice, it will be heralded as "the cancer cure." Encouragingly, further research on mice suggests it may work against many cancers, which could make it truly "*the* cancer cure." Such performance success would make the venture capital investment worth many billions of dollars.

For the aggressive and knowledgeable investor, the many new approaches to cancer represent a compelling opportunity for riches beyond the dreams of avarice. Medicine and medical information carried to the far corners of the earth on the wings of the Internet are a good investment bet.

The Conquest of Aging

Medical science, through discoveries enabled by big data, predictive analytics, and rapid dissemination of that understanding through the Internet, may soon unravel the mechanisms of the aging process. The benefits could be profound. Humans may no longer age nearly so quickly or die so soon. Those with deep insight and wisdom will be around longer, making longer-term contributions.

Efforts toward these momentous developments are already underway in labs and startup companies. Fundamental breakthroughs are likely to occur.

We humans are at an early stage in our evolution, still walking before running toward such discovery, but run we will, all the way to the stars and beyond. This will take a while, though, so in the meantime let's open those venture capital investment checkbooks toward the future.

Acknowledgments

There are so many people to thank that we fear that we'll forget some. For those not identified here, please accept our apologies, along with our sincere thanks.

Our biggest thanks go to our wives, Sharon Batterson and Randy Freeman. Both have lived through multiple decades with the authors, their driven husbands. Just when they thought we were finally slowing down to a normal pace and workload, we decided to write this book to share our knowledge and experience with interested investors and entrepreneurs. Writing a book is a long, hard process. So, Sharon and Randy, thanks for continuing to put up with us!

Our next round of thanks goes to our predecessors and contemporaries in the venture capital industry, from whom we've gained inspiration and knowledge. Thanks as well to the investors who have placed their trust in our team, and to the entrepreneurs we've had the opportunity to work with, from whose shared experiences we've also learned, while having the opportunity at the same time to build wealth for our investors, our colleagues, and our families.

Among this latter group, special gratitude is due to: the late Jim Kimsey and the still very active Steve Case, the individuals most responsible for the tremendous success of AOL, as well as our Harvard Business School classmate George Middlemas, also critical to the startup and development of AOL, which contributed so importantly to Len's career growth; Sanford Morganstein, former president and CEO of the Dytel Corporation, who has so generously shared his venture capital funding experience with our readers; and Chris Gladwin, the founder of Cleversafe, for giving our team its latest opportunity to share in a grand-slam home run success.

A big thanks is due to our VCapital colleagues, who reviewed the book so diligently and thoughtfully and contributed numerous comments and suggestions vital to the final product. Among them is Jim Vaughan, Len's closest business partner for many years and someone who has taught both of us so much about the investors who entrust us with their investment funds. This also includes Fred Tucker, Ryan Kole, Steve Ross, Steve Pedian, and Cindy Lieberman. A big thanks, too, to our VCapital Advisory Board Directors, a group of savvy, successful business experts—Steven Anixter, Tim Danis, Jim Prieur, and Lloyd Shefsky—who are always generous with their inputs and ideas.

Thanks as well to Jon Freeman, Ken's son, a seasoned financial advisor whose counsel encouraged his inherently conservative father to recognize the merits of investing in venture capital. He then reviewed the portion of the book targeted to investors to help keep us totally fair regarding venture capital performance comparisons versus more traditional investment asset classes.

We certainly can't forget about Len's talented assistant, Annie Piotrowski. Thanks to Annie for her essential technical assistance in pulling together all the many pieces that went into this book, some created initially on different software platforms whose ultimate harmonization exceeded our own technical skills.

Finally, we thank our agent, Jeff Herman, and the team at John Wiley & Sons for their belief in the importance of our message for prospective investors and entrepreneurs and their support in making this book happen. In particular, a special thanks goes out to Wiley associates Sharmila Srinivasan and Michael Henton for their vital assistance and support in the design and production steps bringing this book to its ultimate publication.

About the Authors

After preparing for their careers as classmates at the Harvard Business School, the two authors pursued very different paths. Len Batterson pursued a career in venture capital while Ken Freeman pursued a more traditional career in the consumer products and marketing services industries.

Len has been one of the nation's leading entrepreneurial venture capitalists for over 30 years. Beginning his venture capital career in 1982 as an investment analyst with the Venture Capital Division of the Allstate Insurance Company, he served from 1985 to 1987 as the director of Allstate's Venture Capital Division, then one of the nation's oldest, largest, and most successful venture capital management operations. He was responsible for what was at the time one of the largest pools of venture capital in the United States, with more than $350 million invested or committed for investment.

Len's series of notable successes began while at Allstate, where he played an integral role in the financing and restructuring of Control Video Corporation, which became America Online, Inc. (AOL). On its merger with Time Warner, which remains the largest merger in U.S. business history, AOL was valued at $364 billion. While at Allstate, Len also introduced to the venture capital community Allscripts, which was funded by Allstate after Len left the company, and which also grew to unicorn status and still generates over $1 billion in annual revenues.

After leaving Allstate, Len went on to found or co-found a number of highly successful entrepreneurial venture capital funds, pioneering venture capital investment for high-net-worth individuals. His long-term success is exceptional. Len has generated investor returns averaging 28%/year over nearly 30 years, with annual gains in the double digits in every decade, even through the 2000 tech bubble as well as the financial crisis of 2008–09. In addition to AOL and initial involvement with Allscripts, his investments that became unicorns include CyberSource and, more recently, Cleversafe, a data storage innovator sold to IBM in late 2015.

Most recently, Len founded VCapital LLC (www.VCapital.com), providing contemporary online access while continuing to focus on early stage, institutional quality, technology investment opportunities for individual accredited investors.

Ken Freeman began his career with consumer products leader Procter & Gamble in brand management. He went on to serve as vice president of marketing for American Cyanamid's Shulton USA Division (whose iconic brands included Old Spice, Breck, and Pine-Sol) and for the U.S. business of Reckitt & Colman (now Reckitt Benckiser; its vast portfolio of brands included Woolite, Airwick, Easy Off, French's Mustard, and many others) and as vice president, Corporate Marketing Development globally for Nabisco. He subsequently served as president of North American operations for global marketing research leaders NFO (National Family Opinion) and then Taylor Nelson Sofres (TNS).

After leaving TNS in 2006, Ken shifted gears, teaching marketing and corporate finance courses at the undergraduate and graduate school levels at New York's Fashion Institute of Technology. In 2010, he left teaching to join his son in starting up Halston Media, which currently publishes weekly newspapers in four suburban towns in the New York metropolitan area.

Ken caught the venture capital bug in 2014, both as an individual investor and joining with Len to help create VCapital, which he now serves as a strategic advisor. He also serves as nonexecutive chairman of the board of a midsized candy and snack manufacturer and as nonexecutive chairman of his family's newspaper publishing business.

Index